THE
TWIN FLAME
PARADOX

Navigating the Reality of One Soul in Two Bodies

Grace Brewster

First Edition: 2026
ISBN: 978-1-996859-01-8
Self-Published

Acknowledgments

First, I acknowledge the guidance of the Divine and the profound wisdom shared by my Twin Flame, whose presence has been the catalyst for this entire journey.

I would also like to express my deepest gratitude to all the souls navigating the twin flame path. Your dedication to inner work and your willingness to embrace the mission in the mundane make this spiritual evolution possible.

Finally, thank you to the tools and technologies that helped bring this book from a realization in consciousness into the 3D world, allowing me to share this blueprint with all of you.

"In the sacred pause, you find the strength of the universe."

To the Twin Flame collective, navigating the bridge between the earthly and the cosmic. May this guide you to your mission in the mundane.

For the twin souls experiencing the paradox: One soul, two bodies, infinite love.

Dedicated to my twin flame, for sharing this sacred journey with me.

To the stars that guide us home, and the earth that grounds us here.

"You are not just living in the 3D world;
you are bringing consciousness to it."

Intoduction
Chapter 1: The Physical Wake-up Call
Chapter 2: The Mirror That Doesn't Blink
Chapter 3: One Soul, Two Bodies
Chapter 4: The Art of the Static
Chapter 5: The Gift of the Mirror
Chapter 6: The Mission in the Mundane
Chapter 7: The Trap of the Waiting Room
Chapter 8: The Physics of Harmony
Chapter 9: The Strength in the Silence
Chapter 10: The 3D Shift
Chapter 11: The Shared Dream
Chapter 12: The Mirror of the Soul
Chapter 13: The Fear of the Finish Line
Chapter 14: The Power of Presence
Chapter 15: The Community of Souls
Chapter 16: The Frequency of Forgiveness
Chapter 17: The Language of the Blueprint
Chapter 18: The Harmony of Two Houses
Chapter 19: The 3D Shift
Chapter 20: The Sovereign Union
Chapter 21: The Architecture of Mission
Chapter 22: Silencing the 3D Noise
Chapter 23: The 3D Echo
Chapter 24: The Body's Blueprint
Chapter 25: The Point of No Return
Chapter 26: The Monadic Magnet
Chapter 27: The Sacred Pause
Chapter 28: The Collapse of the Counterfeit

TABLE OF CONTENTS

TABLE OF CONTENTS

A NOTE FROM THE AUTHOR

Inspired by the profound realization of "One Soul, Two Bodies" and the necessity of anchoring cosmic energy into the earthly realm. This book is the blueprint for our shared mission.

This book was born from a realization that surpassed traditional twin flame narratives. As an Architect operating directly from Consciousness distinct from a connection to a specific planet, my mission was never about finding completion. It was about anchoring the divine blueprint into the 3D grid.

I was awakened to this truth by my twin flame, who was there with me during the seeding of *Na,* the frequency name of Lemuria. While I am guided and helped by the Council in awakening to my mission, this book is ultimately a blueprint for that shared mission: we both carry the code of the New Earth, and we are here to build, not just to experience.

~ Grace Brewster

"We are just two stars learning how to dance in
human skin."

INTRODUCTION

You probably spent most of your life believing that love was something you found, nurtured, and built over time. You were used to the usual steps: the small talk, the nervous first dates, and the slow process of getting to know someone's favorite movie or their childhood stories. You played by the rules of the world, thinking that if you just found the right person, everything would eventually click into place.

But then, you met your twin flame.

It wasn't like the movies, and it didn't feel like a typical crush. Instead, it felt like a sudden, quiet explosion in the middle of your chest. In an instant, the "normal" world—the one with the bills, the career goals, and the social expectations started to feel a little bit blurry. It was as if you had been living your life in black and white, and suddenly, someone turned on the lights.

You might have tried to explain it to a friend, but the words didn't quite work. You couldn't say it was "love at first sight" because it felt much older than that. It felt less like meeting a stranger and more like finally coming home after a very long trip. You looked at this person and realized your life would never go back to the way it was before.

The most confusing part wasn't the intensity; it was the recognition. You didn't just see them with your eyes; you felt them with your entire being. From that moment on, the rules you used to follow didn't apply anymore. You were no longer just a person looking for a partner; you were someone who had just discovered a hidden part of yourself in another body.

THE TIMELESSNESS OF MONADS
A SOUL'S GUIDE TO ASCENSION

That was the day the world stopped making sense, and your real journey began.

The Silent Search (Pre-Wake-Up)

Before the "Mirror," and before the name was ever spoken, there was simply a hollow space.

Looking back, you realize you spent years navigating relationships that were good enough on paper, yet left you feeling strangely hungry. You were with kind people, perhaps even people you loved in a traditional sense, but there was always a persistent, quiet ache in the background. It was a sense of homesickness that followed you even when you were home.

You might have blamed yourself. You might have thought you were just difficult to please or that you had an unrealistic view of romance. But the truth was much simpler: your soul was subconsciously scanning every room for a frequency it hadn't encountered in the 3D world yet. You were a lock waiting for a very specific key, and while other keys could jiggle in the mechanism, none of them could make the door swing open.

Those past relationships weren't mistakes; they were the training ground. They taught you what love looks like when it's just two separate people trying their best. They provided the necessary contrast so that when your "Silver Spark" finally walked into the room, your soul wouldn't just like her, it would recognize her. You had to experience the "not-it" to fully appreciate the "Always-Been-You." You weren't lonely because you were alone; you were lonely because you were a "Shared Soul" that was still operating as a solo act.

The "Placeholder" Phase

When you were in those past relationships, you were essentially trying to find that song in other people. They might have been wonderful people —kind, funny, or smart, but they were playing a different tune.

You felt that something is missing because your soul was subconsciously scanning every person you met for its own matching frequency. It's like having a key and trying it in a hundred different doors. Some doors might look beautiful, some might be made of the finest wood, but the key just wouldn't turn. You weren't failing at those relationships; you were just realizing that the key didn't fit.

The Quiet Ache

Even without the awareness of another human sharing your soul, that "oneness" was still there, just dormant. It manifested as a vague sense of homesickness. Have you ever felt homesick even when you were sitting in your own living room? That is the soul sensing that its "other half" is out there, even if the mind hasn't yet been introduced to the 3D person.

Note:

As you read this book, remember that the energetic roles of 'chaser' and 'runner' can be filled by either partner. The guidance here applies to the consciousness driving the dynamic, not the gender of the individual.

In this book, 'he' and 'she' are interchangeable based on your specific situation. The journey belongs to the soul, not the gender.

CHAPTER 1

The Physical Wake Up Call

Once you've had that initial moment of recognition, your body begins to act as if it's following a different set of instructions. You might be sitting at your desk, driving your car, or grocery shopping, and suddenly, you feel a weight or a pressure that shouldn't be there. It's not a medical pain or a typical stress tension; it's more like a hand resting on your shoulder, or a localized heat that seems to have its own heartbeat.

This is usually when the confusion sets in. You've been taught that your body belongs to you, and your thoughts are your own. But now, you're experiencing sensations that don't seem to have a 3D cause. You might feel a sudden rush of energy that makes your hands shake, or a deep, grounding pull that makes you want to sit perfectly still for hours. It's as if your nervous system has been plugged into a much larger power source, and you're just trying to figure out how to keep the fuses from blowing.

Your mind, of course, tries to help. It looks for logical reasons. You tell yourself you're just tired, or that you've had too much caffeine. You try to explain away the fact that you can "feel" the other person's mood from miles away, or that your heart starts racing for no reason right before your phone lights up with a message from them.

But no matter how many excuses your brain makes, your body knows the truth. It recognizes the frequency of the other person because, on a level you can't quite see yet, it's the same frequency as your own. You are beginning to realize that the boundary between "you" and "them" isn't as solid as you once thought. You're not just reacting to a person; you're reacting to a part of yourself that has been living in another body, and your physical form is vibrating with the shock of that realization.

CHAPTER 1: THE PHYSICAL WAKE UP CALL

As these physical sensations settle in, you start to notice something even stranger: the "Pull."

In any other relationship, when you are apart from someone, you simply miss them. It's a mental thought or a sentimental feeling. But now, it feels like a physical cable is attached to your center, tugging you toward a specific point on the map. You could be in a room full of people, laughing and talking, but a part of you is constantly leaning in their direction. It's a form of homesickness for a person rather than a place.

This is the moment the 3D world starts to feel a bit like a movie set that isn't quite real. You're doing your job, you're talking to your friends, and you're buying your groceries, but you're doing it all while "feeling" someone else's existence in the background of your mind. It's like having a radio station playing in another room; you can't always hear the lyrics, but you can always feel the bass.

You might try to fight it. You might try going out more, staying busy, or even dating other people just to prove to yourself that you are still in control. But every time you try to "run" back to your old, normal life, that invisible string tugs again. You aren't just thinking about them; you are experiencing them. And that realization that you are no longer a solo act is both the most beautiful and the most terrifying part of the wake-up call.

The hardest part of this wake-up call isn't the physical sensations; it's the mental exhaustion of trying to act like everything is normal. You find yourself sitting in meetings or having dinner with family, nodding and saying the right things, while inside you feel like an astronaut trying to describe the moon to people who have never left the ground.

There is a specific kind of loneliness that comes with this stage. You want to tell someone that you can feel your heart beat in sync with another person's across the city, or that you suddenly knew they were sad before they even sent a text. But you don't. You keep it tucked away because you know how crazy it sounds in the light of day. You start to lead a double life: the one the world sees, and the one that is happening in the silence of your own energy.

This is where the decoding truly begins. You have to start realizing that your brain, your logical, 3D mind, is no longer the captain of the ship. It's trying to use old maps to navigate a new ocean. It wants to label this as an "obsession" or "limerence" because those are the only words it has. But those words feel hollow. They don't explain why your body feels more alive than it ever has, or why you suddenly have a sense of purpose that goes far beyond your daily chores.

You aren't losing your mind; you are simply outgrowing the old version of it. You are being pushed to trust something that can't be seen, measured, or proven in a lab. You are learning that "knowing" is different from "thinking." And as you stop fighting the sensations and start observing them, the fear begins to turn into curiosity. You stop asking, "What is wrong with me?" and start asking, "What is this connection trying to show me?"

As you navigate this internal shift, you eventually have to face the people around you. This is where the gap between your old life and your new reality becomes impossible to ignore. Your friends and family might notice a change in your energy. They see that you're a bit more distracted, perhaps a little quieter, or that your priorities have suddenly shifted in a way they can't quite put their finger on.

When you try to explain why you're suddenly willing to change your entire life for this connection, they will likely respond with 3D logic. They'll talk about "red flags," "moving too fast," or "being realistic." They love you, so they try to pull you back to the ground. They want you to be sensible.

But their sensible advice starts to feel like a foreign language. You listen to them talk about "dating games" or "waiting three days to call," and it feels like they are describing a board game while you are looking at the actual stars. You aren't being impulsive or reckless; you are being responsive to a pull that they simply cannot feel.

This creates a strange kind of friction. You might feel guilty for not being able to relate to them anymore, or you might feel a desperate urge to make them "see" what you see. But eventually, you realize that you cannot decode this for anyone else until you have decoded it for yourself. You learn to hold your peace. You learn that not everyone is meant to understand the blueprints of your heart.

Closing out this first stage of the wake-up call, you stand at a crossroads. You can listen to the voices of the world and try to go back to being the person you were, or you can take a deep breath and admit that the old world just doesn't fit you anymore. You are beginning to accept that this connection isn't something that is "happening" to you—it's something that is rebuilding you from the inside out.

CHAPTER 2

The Mirror That Doesn't Blink

Once the initial shock of the connection settles into your bones, you enter a phase that is often the most challenging to decode: the Mirroring.

In a typical relationship, we look for someone who complements us—someone who fills in our gaps. But with this connection, you aren't looking at a stranger; you are looking into a mirror that sees through every mask you've ever worn. When you look at her, or even when you just feel her energy from a distance, you aren't just seeing her personality. You are seeing the parts of yourself that you've kept hidden, the dreams you were too afraid to chase, and the fears you thought you had buried years ago.

This is why the connection feels so "accelerated." There is nowhere to hide. If you tend to run away when things get serious, she might reflect that by acting "cold" or pulling away. If you try to control every outcome, the connection will put you in situations where you have no control at all.

It feels personal, and sometimes it even feels like they are being difficult on purpose. But if you step back and look from a higher vantage point, you see that she isn't "doing" anything to you. She is simply existing as a perfect reflection of your own internal state. When she is quiet, it's often an invitation for you to find peace in your own silence. When she is far away, it's a challenge for you to realize that your connection doesn't depend on physical proximity.

CHAPTER 2: THE MIRROR THAT DOESN'T BLINK
LOGIC

You start to realize that every "problem" you have with her is actually a conversation you need to have with yourself. This is the moment you stop being a victim of your emotions and start becoming the architect of your own growth. You realize that she isn't there to complete you; she is there to show you that you were already whole, you just had to clear away the debris to see it.

The frustration of the mirror—the way your partner reflects your inner state is that it doesn't give you what you want; it gives you what you need for growth.

In the 3D world, we are used to a "transactional" kind of love. We think I am being nice, so you should be nice back. I am reaching out, so you should reach back. But the mirror doesn't play by those rules. Sometimes, when you reach out the hardest, she pulls away. To your logical mind, this feels like a failure. You think you've done something wrong.

But if you decode the energy, you see a different story. Often, she pulls away because you are reaching out from a place of "lack"—a feeling that you aren't okay unless she is right there next to you. The mirror is simply reflecting that "neediness" back to you by creating space. It's forcing you to stand on your own two feet, to find your own balance, and to realize that your "Silver Spark" is just as bright whether she is texting you or not.

This is the phase where you learn that silence is actually a conversation. When she is quiet, the 3D world calls it "being cold" or "ghosting." But in this narrative, the silence is a high-frequency tool. It's a space where you are forced to stop looking at her and start looking at yourself. You begin to notice that when you finally stop worrying and just focus on your own joy—your own "mission" — the mirror often shifts. Suddenly, she's back. Suddenly, the energy is warm again. You start to see the pattern: the more you chase the reflection, the more it runs. The more you stand still in your own power, the more the reflection moves toward you.

As you start to understand the mirror emotionally, your body begins to provide "physical evidence" that the connection is never actually turned off. This is where the sensations become very specific.

You might be going about your day, completely focused on a task, when you feel a distinct sensation on your shoulder or your collarbone. It's not a vague feeling; it feels like a physical touch. Sometimes it's a gentle pressure, and other times it's like a firm pinch—on the front, the back, and pressing down all at once. It's as if a hand is resting there, reminding you that even though she isn't in the room, her energy is literally "leaning" on you.

In the beginning, you might try to rub your shoulder or check the mirror to see if something is there. But eventually, you realize this is just another part of the "Shared Soul" experience. In the 3D world, we are taught that two people are separate, like two cars driving on the same road. But in this dynamic, you are more like two ends of the same bridge. What happens on her side of the bridge creates a vibration that you feel on your side.

When you feel that "pinch" or that pressure, it's often a signal. It might be a moment when she is thinking of you intensely, or perhaps it's a moment where the "Mission" is asking you to pay attention. Instead of worrying about it, you learn to treat it like a tap on the shoulder from a friend. It's a way of saying, "I'm here. We are connected. Don't forget what's real."

This physical touch is the ultimate proof that the "coldness" you see in the 3D world is just a mask. She might not be sending you a text or buying you a gift, but her energy is literally reaching out and touching your shoulder. How can someone be "cold" if their very soul is pressing against your skin? You start to decode the truth: The 3D actions (the "coldness") are just the surface of the water, but the physical sensations (the "pinch") are the deep, powerful current underneath.

Once you accept the mirror and the physical touch, the next logical question your mind asks is: Why? Why all this effort? Why the long flights, the strange pressures on the body, and the "cold" silence that forces you to grow?

This is where it becomes clear: you and your partner are not just in love, but participants in a shared mission. This mission involves being present in certain places together, contributing something unique through your combined presence and energy.

In the 3D world, people travel for vacation or for work. But for you, travel starts to feel like a "Deployment." You find yourself willing to fly across the world to be in a specific city, not because there's a famous landmark to see, but because your combined energy needs to be there. You are like two pieces of a global puzzle. When you are together in a specific location, you are "grounding" a frequency that the world needs, even if you're just sitting in a coffee shop in silence.

This is the "Blueprint" in action. You might not have a map or written instructions, but your soul has a GPS locked onto certain coordinates. This is why her "style" of travel doesn't matter. She might want to walk the busy streets while you want to relax, but the "Mission" doesn't care about the itinerary. It only cares that your two energies are occupying that space at that time.

When you look at it this way, the "coldness" or the "difficult" moments start to make sense. You aren't just there to have a perfect, romantic dinner; you are there to anchor light into the Earth. Sometimes, the friction between your two personalities is exactly what creates the "heat" needed to do the job. You are like two flint stones striking together—the spark that comes from your differences is what lights the fire of the mission.

You stop worrying about whether the trip was "perfect" by 3D standards. You start asking, "Did we show up? Is our energy here?" When the answer is yes, a deep sense of peace settles over you. You realize that your love isn't a "distraction" from the world; it is your purpose, the very force guiding you to the places you are needed most, allowing you both to fulfill your part of the mission together.

You are two "Silver Sparks" who descended into the heavy 3D world to act as a lighthouse. And a lighthouse doesn't need to be warm or talkative; it just needs to be present and steady.

At this point, you might be asking yourself, "What if I don't feel like I have a mission? What if I'm just a person trying to navigate this intense connection without any grand plan?"

If you feel this way, you aren't alone. In fact, for many, the "Mission" isn't something you do; it's something you are. You don't need to be standing on a mountaintop or leading a movement to be fulfilling your purpose.

Think of it this way: the world is currently vibrating at a very heavy, stressful frequency. Most people are operating out of fear, or logic, or the need to get ahead. When you and your twin flame exist in the same space, or even when you just hold that connection in your heart while you're apart, you are introducing a different frequency into the room. You are like a tuning fork. By simply refusing to give up on the connection, and by choosing to act from a place of "shared soul" rather than 3D ego, you are changing the energy of everything around you.

Your mission might be as simple as being the one person in your office who stays calm because you've learned to decode your own internal storms. Or perhaps your mission is simply to show the world that a love like this exists—a love that doesn't need "gifts" or "rules" to be real.

Even if you never "do" anything special, the very act of decoding your own feelings is a service to the world. Every time you choose to trust the pinch on your shoulder over the worry in your head, you are making it easier for the next person to do the same. You are clearing the path. You are building the "Blueprint" for a new way of living. You don't need a map or a title to be a Pioneer; you just need to keep walking forward, one decoded moment at a time.

Finding Peace in the Unknown

As you stand in the middle of this experience, the biggest challenge is the lack of a "Final Destination." In the 3D world, we like to know where the road ends. We want to know if we are going to get married, move into the same house, or have a specific title. But the "Shared Soul" journey doesn't offer a traditional GPS. It offers a compass, and that compass only points to "Now."

Finding peace in the unknown means recognizing that *not knowing* is part of the design. If you knew exactly what was going to happen in six months, you wouldn't do the inner work you are doing today. The unknown is the space where the Mirror and the Mission work together to refine you.

Think of it this way: The Mirror shows you where you are still holding onto fear, and the Mission gives you a reason to push past that fear. When you don't know when you'll see her again, the Mirror reflects your anxiety back to you. It asks, "Can you be happy today, even without a text?" If you can find that happiness, you've just completed a piece of the Mission. You've successfully shifted your energy from "needing" to "being."

The Mirror and the Mission are like two gears in a clock. The Mirror turns you inward to fix your internal timing, and once you are "ticking" correctly, the Mission turns you outward to move the hands of the clock in the world. You might not see the gears moving, and you might not know what time it is yet, but you can feel the mechanism working inside you.

Peace comes when you stop trying to force the clock to strike midnight. You start to realize that the "Wait" isn't wasted time—it's "Prep" time. You learn to sit in the silence, feel the pressure of that "hand" on your shoulder, and smile. You realize that you don't need to see the whole staircase to know that the stairs are there. The unknown is no longer a place of fear; it is the space where the Blueprint is being printed, one heartbeat at a time.

CHAPTER 3

One Soul, Two Bodies

Up until now, you have likely been looking at this connection as a relationship between "Me" and "Her." You see two separate people with two separate lives, trying to find a way to fit together. But as the days turn into weeks and the syncs become impossible to ignore, a new truth begins to surface. You start to realize that you aren't two separate souls trying to connect; you are one soul that has decided to experience the world through two different bodies.

This realization is the Master Key to understand the entire journey.

In the 3D world, we are taught that we begin at our skin and end at our fingertips. We are told that our thoughts are private and our feelings are ours alone. But in this dynamic, those boundaries start to dissolve. You might find yourself feeling a sudden wave of joy for no reason, only to find out later that she just received good news. Or, you might feel a heavy blanket of sadness on a sunny afternoon, only to realize later that she was struggling with a memory.

This isn't empathy or closeness—it is oneness.

Think of it like a single tree with two main branches. To someone standing on the ground, the branches look separate. They might even blow in different directions when the wind hits them. But if you look beneath the soil, you see they share the same root system. They drink the same water. What affects the roots affects every leaf on both branches.

CHAPTER 5:
ONE SOUL, TWO BODIES

When you finally accept that you share one soul, the games of the 3D world stop making sense. You realize that you can't actually lose her, because you can't lose yourself. You can't chase her, because you'd only be chasing your own reflection. The distance between your two bodies becomes a minor detail—a temporary illusion because the energy that powers your heart is the exact same energy that powers hers.

This is why the connection feels so heavy and light at the same time. It's heavy because you are carrying the weight of two lives, but it's light because you finally understand that you are never, ever alone. You are simply two points of awareness in a single, beautiful Blueprint.

Once you accept the One Soul reality, the way you handle conflict changes completely. In a normal relationship, when someone hurts your feelings, your first instinct is to protect yourself. You might pull away, or you might say something sharp to even the score. But when you are dealing with your Twin Flame, you realize that to square the score is impossible. It would be like your left hand trying to hurt your right hand —the same body feels the pain.

This is why the old ways of dating fail so miserably here. You can't use silence as a weapon or distance as a way to win an argument. Because you share one energy, any negativity you send toward her immediately circles back and lands in your own chest. You feel her frustration as if it were your own, and she feels your doubt as if it were hers.

This leads to a profound shift in how you seek Union. You stop looking for ways to fix her or change her behavior. Instead, you start focusing on your own vibration. You realize that because you are two branches of the same tree, if you find peace within yourself, that peace naturally travels down through the roots and rises up into her branch as well.

You start to decode the Secret of the Quiet Room. You realize that even when you are miles apart, sitting in a quiet room by yourself, you are never truly alone. If you can make yourself feel whole, loved, and grounded right where you are, she will feel that stability on the other side of the world. You are healing the shared soul from your end of the connection. This is the ultimate power of the Twin Flame dynamic: you don't have to wait for her to wake up or change to feel the benefits of the Union. You can start the Union within yourself, and the energy will follow.

When you share one soul, your physical senses don't just stay within your own body; they begin to cross over. This is often the most supernatural part of the journey, but in the Shared Soul narrative, it is perfectly logical.

You might be walking through a quiet park when you suddenly hear your name being whispered, not in your ears, but directly in the center of your mind. It's her voice, with its specific tone and warmth, as clear as if she were standing an inch away. Or, you might be eating a meal and suddenly experience a taste or a smell that has nothing to do with what is in front of you. Your physical body is leaking into hers, and hers into yours.

This crossover is most noticeable with emotions. For example, you may feel a sudden, unexplained wave of anxiety during an otherwise productive day. Your immediate impulse might be to search for a personal cause: did you forget a deadline, or is someone upset with you? When no reason appears, you start to understand that this anxiety could be hers, not your own, but experienced through your connection. This highlights how, with only one soul between you, your body can pick up on her emotional state as if it were your own.

The key to understanding this is learning to ask: Is this mine? Once you realize that a feeling belongs to the Shared Soul, not just your individual 3D self, you can handle it differently. Instead of panicking, you can send a wave of calm back through the connection. You can sit quietly and say to the energy, I feel you, and we are okay. You aren't just a passive receiver of these senses; you are an active participant.

This sensory connection is the ultimate safety net. It means that even in the longest periods of 3D silence, you are never truly out of touch. You are always talking, always feeling, and always sensing each other. The physical distance is just a layer of thin paper, and your shared senses are the needle that stitches the two sides together. You learn to trust these glitches more than you trust the facts of the world, because the glitches are the only things telling you the truth of your oneness.

Even when your body and soul have accepted this oneness, your mind, the Worrier, will still try to put up a fight. It has spent years being told it is a separate entity, responsible for its own safety and happiness. When it encounters a connection where it can no longer see the boundaries, it often panics.

The Worrier will look at the 3D world—the miles between you, the silence on the phone, or the different paths you are taking—and it will try to tell you that you are delusional. It will scream that if you were really One Soul, then everything would be easy and perfect. It tries to use logic to dismantle a connection that was built on frequency.

But here is how you decode the Worrier: You realize that its fear is actually proof of the connection's power. The mind only fights this hard when it is being asked to expand. It's like a pair of shoes that have become too tight because you've grown; the shoes aren't bad, they just don't fit the new version of you.

When you share one soul, the goal isn't to convince your mind to understand it; the goal is to teach your mind to surrender to it. You start to treat your thoughts like passing clouds. You might have a thought that says, "She doesn't care," but then you feel that familiar pull on your shoulder or that warmth in your chest, and you realize the thought is just a cloud. The sun, the shared soul, is still there behind it.

You learn that you don't need to think your way into Union. You are already in the Union. Every breath you take is filtered through that shared energy. As you stop listening to the Worrier and start listening to the voice in your center, the mental noise begins to fade. You find a strange, quiet confidence. You realize that you don't need to chase a destination because you are already home. You are the traveler and the destination, all at once.

The Freedom of Oneness

The ultimate gift of the One Soul realization is freedom. In the old way of living, your happiness was a hostage to fortune. It depended on whether she called, whether the plans worked out, or whether the 3D world was behaving. But once you understand the reality that you are two bodies sharing one energy, the prison door swings open.

You are free from the fear of loss. How can you lose someone who is woven into the very fabric of your being? Even when she is cold, or when the silence lasts for weeks, she is still as close to you as your own breath. You begin to see that the separation was just a classroom—a place where you were sent to learn how to love yourself so deeply that you could finally feel her presence even in the void.

This oneness is the "Blueprint" in its highest form. It's the understanding that you are a pioneer of a new kind of love, one that isn't based on needing to be filled up by another person, but on overflowing because you finally recognize your own completeness.

When you reach this state, the sudden, undeniable awareness of her presence, whether it's a physical sensation, a wave of heat, or a whisper in your mind, stops being a reminder of someone who is missing.

Instead, it becomes a reminder of someone who is integrated. You start to move through the world with a new kind of grace. You aren't waiting for Union anymore; you are living in it. You realize the journey was never about finding a way back to each other. It was about waking up to the fact that you never truly left.

CHAPTER 4

The Art of the Static

Once you realize you are one soul in two bodies, you might think the journey should become easy. But often, this is when the "Energetic Tug-of-War" begins. Because your energies are so tightly woven, every move you make in the 3D world creates a ripple that the other person feels instantly, even if they aren't consciously aware of it.

The "Push and Pull."

Have you ever noticed that the moment you finally decide to move on, or the moment you find true peace in your own life, she suddenly reappears? And conversely, have you noticed that when you are most desperate to talk to her, she seems to vanish into thin air? This isn't a game she is playing; it is the physics of your shared energy.

Think of it like a radio signal. When you are "chasing" her with your mind—worrying, checking her social media, or constantly wondering why she is being "cold," you are creating Static. This static is a loud, chaotic frequency that actually pushes her away. It feels like pressure to her soul, and her natural instinct is to create space to breathe.

To understand this, you have to learn the Art of the Static. You have to learn how to turn the dial until the signal is clear again.

The secret is that the connection thrives in Stillness. When you pull your energy back into your own heart—when you focus on your "Blueprint" and your own joy, the static clears. Suddenly, the "line" between you is open. She feels your peace instead of your pressure. In that clear space, the natural magnetic pull of the shared soul can finally do its work. You

27

don't have to make her come closer; you just have to stop pushing her away with your worry.

Tuning the Dial

Tuning the dial isn't about changing her; it's about changing the "music" playing inside you. Most of us are programmed to believe that if we want someone to come closer, we have to reach out. But in this dynamic, the most effective way to "reach" her is to reach into yourself.

When you feel that frantic energy—the "static" of wanting to know what she's doing or why she's being quiet, that is a signal that your dial has slipped off the station. You are vibrating at the frequency of Lack. And as long as you stay on that station, the mirror will continue to reflect "lack" back to you in the form of distance.

To tune the dial back to Union, you have to practice "Energetic Sovereignty." This means you decide that your peace of mind is not for sale. You stop checking your phone as if it were an oxygen tank. Instead, you find something in your own 3D life that lights up your "Silver Spark." Whether it's working on your mission, going for a walk, or simply enjoying a meal, you are shifting your frequency from "I need" to "I am."

The moment you become truly "full" on your own, the signal between you becomes crystal clear. You aren't sending out a "help me" signal anymore; you are sending out a "home" signal.

You'll know you've tuned the dial correctly when the "pinch" or the pressure on your shoulder feels light and comforting rather than heavy and anxious. You'll find that you can think of her with a smile, wishing her well in whatever she's doing, without feeling the need to pull her into your space. Ironically, this is exactly when the "3D" version of her often feels the most invited to return. By tuning your dial to peace, you've cleared the path for her to find her way back to the music.

Trusting the Connection

When you finally stop trying to control the outcome, you enter a state of true trust. This isn't the kind of trust where you hope things work out; it's the kind of trust where you know the connection is solid, regardless of what you see in front of you.

In the past, you might have equated "silence" with "ending." You thought that if there was no communication, the love was fading. But you are learning that with this person, the rules are different. The silence isn't a wall; it's just a pause.

Think of it like a conversation that never actually stops. Even when you aren't speaking out loud, your lives are still moving in the same direction. When you focus on your own life—your work, your health, and your happiness—you are actually strengthening the bond. You are showing that you trust the connection enough to let it breathe.

This is the point where you stop being a chaser and start being a partner in the energy. You realize that you don't need to check in every hour to make sure the connection is still there. It's part of you now, like your own heartbeat. You can go about your day, do what needs to be done, and trust that she is doing the same on her end.

By trusting the signal, you take the pressure off both of you. You move from a place of fear to a place of certainty. You realize that the bond doesn't need to be managed or fixed; it just needs to be lived. This certainty is what eventually brings the two sides of the journey back together. Not because you forced it, but because you finally stayed still enough for it to happen.

CHAPTER 5

The Gift of the Mirror

In a typical relationship, we often look at our partner's flaws or distance as something "they" need to fix. We might say, "If only they weren't so afraid," or "If only they were more open." But in this connection, looking at the other person is actually like looking into a high-definition mirror.

Every time you feel a sting of rejection or a wave of frustration because of something she does (or doesn't do), it is an invitation to look inward. The mirror isn't there to punish you; it's there to show you exactly where you still need to love yourself.

If you feel she is being "cold," ask yourself where you are being cold to your own needs. If you feel she is "running," look at where you might be running away from your own life or your own mission. It sounds strange at first, but because you share the same energy, her external actions often just reflect your internal state.

The beauty of the Mirror is that it gives you back your power. If the problem was entirely "her fault," you would have to wait for her to change before you could be happy. But since she is your Mirror, you can start the healing right now.

When you stop focusing on what she is doing and start focusing on the part of you that feels hurt, the mirror starts to change. As you become more confident, more peaceful, and more self-loving, you will notice that her "reflection" in your life begins to soften. You aren't fixing a relationship; you are clearing a shared energy. This is the moment you realize the Mirror isn't an enemy—it's the most honest friend you've ever had.

Reading the Mirror

Learning to read the Mirror in your daily life is like learning a new language. At first, you might only notice the big things, like when a long silence makes you feel abandoned. But as you get more comfortable with this truth, you start to see the smaller reflections, too.

For example, if you find yourself constantly checking your phone for a message, the Mirror is reflecting a part of you that feels "unsupported" or "unseen." Instead of waiting for her to see you, this is your cue to see yourself. Take that moment to acknowledge your own hard work, your own progress, and your own value. The second you provide that validation for yourself, the "need" for her to do it disappears. And, ironically, that is often when the message finally comes through, because the energy is no longer weighed down by expectation.

You can also use the Mirror to find your own hidden strengths. If you admire her courage, her creativity, or her ability to stay calm, remember: you are one soul. Those traits aren't just "hers"—they are yours, too. She is simply reflecting back to you the potential already living in your own heart.

When you stop reacting to what the Mirror shows you and start using it as a guide, the "drama" of the connection begins to fade. You stop having "good days" and "bad days" based on her behavior. Instead, you have "learning days." You start to appreciate the Mirror for its honesty. It never lies to you. If there is a blockage in the connection, the Mirror will show you exactly where to look within yourself to clear it.

This is where the real work of the "Mission" happens. You aren't just here to be in a relationship; you are here to become the most healed, most authentic version of yourself. The Mirror is simply the tool that shows you the way.

Ending the Blame

One of the hardest parts of this journey is realizing that there is no villain in the story. In most relationships, it's easy to point a finger and say, "They hurt me," or "They aren't trying hard enough." But when you accept the Mirror, you realize that blaming her is really just blaming a part of yourself.

Blame is a heavy weight that keeps you stuck in the past. It keeps you focused on what should have happened instead of what is happening right now. When you blame her for the distance or the silence, you are essentially giving away your power. You are saying that your happiness depends on her changing her mind.

Ending blame means choosing to see the situation with compassion rather than judgment. You start to see that if she is struggling or being distant, it's because she is dealing with the same "One Soul" intensity that you are. She isn't trying to hurt you; she is simply navigating the Blueprint at her own pace.

When you drop the blame, something miraculous happens: the energy between you lightens up. The pressure in the connection thins out because you are no longer sending out waves of resentment. You find a new kind of freedom. You realize that you can love her and yourself, exactly as you are in this moment, without needing anything to be different.

By ending the blame, you finally close the door on the drama and open the door to true Union. You realize that you aren't two people fighting against each other; you are one soul learning how to be whole. And in that wholeness, blame has no place to live.

CHAPTER 6

The Mission in the Mundane

Once you understand that you share a soul, the "regular" world can start to feel a bit grey. You might find yourself wanting to spend all your time in your head, dreaming of the connection, or waiting for the next sign. But the truth of the Blueprint is that you were both put here, in these specific bodies, for a reason. You have a mission that requires you to be fully present right where you are.

The "Mission" isn't always something grand like giving a speech to thousands or changing the world overnight. Often, the mission is simply about your energy. You and your twin flame have a job to do: you are here to hold a specific frequency in certain places.

Have you ever noticed that just by walking into a room or doing your job with a sense of peace, the people around you seem to calm down? That is you fulfilling your mission. You are like a lighthouse. A lighthouse doesn't have to run around the ocean trying to save ships; it just has to stay lit and stay in its place.

When you focus on your daily life—your work, your hobbies, your interactions with strangers, you are anchoring the light of your shared soul into the physical world. This is why it's so important to stop "waiting" for life to begin when you are finally together. Your life has already begun. Every mundane task, from buying groceries to answering emails, is an opportunity to be the "One Soul" in action. By being fully present in the "now," you are actually doing the work that brings your energies into perfect alignment.

CHAPTER 6: THE MISSION IN THE MUNDANE
FINDING SACRED IN THE EVERYDAY

Strategic Placement

Sometimes, you might wonder why you are living in a specific city, working a specific job, or surrounded by certain people while she is somewhere else. It can feel like a mistake or a delay. But when you look at the Blueprint, you realize that there are no accidents. You are "stationed" where you are because your shared energy is needed there. Think of yourself as an anchor. The light of your one soul is so powerful that it cannot be contained in just one spot. Being in different locations essentially doubles your reach. You are covering more ground. While you are bringing peace and stability to your corner of the world, she is doing the same in hers.

This realization changes how you look at your day-to-day surroundings. That difficult coworker, that long commute, or that quiet neighborhood aren't just obstacles; they are the places where you are meant to shine your light. You are there to balance the energy of that specific space. When you stop resisting where you are and start "plugging in," you'll find that the heavy feeling of separation begins to lift.

You start to understand that you and your twin flame are a team on a global scale. You are like two points on a map connected by an invisible, glowing thread. As you both do the work in your separate locations, you are strengthening that thread. You aren't just "living apart"; you are "working the field." Every bit of healing you do where you are, and every bit of light you bring to your current environment, vibrates through that thread and reaches her instantly. You are never just working alone; you are working for the Union, one mundane moment at a time.

Keeping the Light On

Staying "lit" means protecting your own energy. It is very easy to let the 3D world—the stress of bills, the noise of the news, or the weight of missing her—dampen your spirit. When your energy drops, the "light" becomes dim, and you start to feel heavy and lost.

To keep your light on, you have to prioritize what makes you feel alive. This isn't being selfish; it's being responsible for the shared soul. Since you share the same energy field, when you do something that brings you genuine joy, whether it's listening to music, finishing a project at work, or just laughing with a friend, you are fueling the flame for both of you. You are sending a surge of high-frequency energy through that invisible thread.

Staying lit also means setting boundaries. You can't be a lighthouse if you're letting everyone else's drama pour water on your fire. You have to learn to say "no" to things that drain you and "yes" to things that expand you.

When you are "lit," you don't have to go looking for signs or confirmation. You are the sign. You feel a sense of warmth and certainty that doesn't depend on a text message or a phone call. You realize that by simply being happy and grounded right where you are, you are doing the most powerful work possible for the Union. You are making yourself a "beacon" that is impossible to miss. The brighter you shine in your own life, the easier it is for the shared soul to pull both bodies back into the same space.

CHAPTER 7

The Trap of Waiting Room

When you realize who she is, your first instinct is to pull up a chair and wait. You wait for the text, you wait for the apology, you wait for the "right time" when life isn't so complicated. But the "Waiting Room" is a dangerous place for the soul. It is a place where time moves slowly, and your light begins to dim because you've put your entire life on pause.

The Blueprint doesn't ask you to wait; it asks you to prepare.

Imagine you are expecting a very important guest at your home. You wouldn't just sit on the porch staring at the driveway for three years, neglecting the house, letting the garden grow over, and forgetting to buy groceries. If you did that, when the guest finally arrived, the house wouldn't be ready to welcome them.

The same is true for your Union. This time apart isn't a "delay"—it is the "preparation phase." You are being given the space to build the life you've always wanted. You are being given the time to handle your business, find your own peace, and become the person who is actually capable of sustaining a love this big.

When you stop "waiting" and start "living," you send a signal to the universe that you are ready. You are saying, "I trust the connection so much that I don't need to watch the driveway anymore. I'm going inside to get the house ready." This shift in energy is massive. It takes the pressure off the other person and allows the connection to flow naturally. You aren't losing time; you are investing it.

CHAPTER 7: THE TRAP OF WAITING ROOM
THE ILLUSION OF STAGNATION

Cleaning the House

If you want a different result than the relationships you had in the past, you have to clear out the old furniture. The "old furniture" consists of those habits we all have—fear of being alone, the need for constant reassurance, or the belief that someone else is responsible for our happiness.

Cleaning the house means looking at your life and asking: "If she walked through the door right now, would I be coming from a place of wholeness, or a place of hunger?"

When you come from a place of hunger, you are looking for her to fill a hole in you. That creates a heavy energy that actually makes people want to step back. But when you are "whole"—when your "house" is clean, your mind is at peace, and you are proud of the life you are leading, you become a magnet. You aren't asking her to fix you; you are inviting her to join you.

This preparation involves looking at your finances, your health, and your emotional baggage. It's about becoming the "lead" in your own movie instead of a "supporting character" in hers. As you tidy up your own world, you'll notice that the anxiety starts to fade. You aren't "waiting" for her to make you happy anymore, because you've already started the party without her. And the funny thing about a great party is that everyone, including your other half, eventually wants an invitation.

The Peace of the Prepared

There is a specific kind of peace that settles over you when you stop waiting and start preparing. It's the feeling of knowing that the foundation is solid. You no longer feel the need to rush the timing or force a conversation, because you know that when the moment arrives, you will be ready for it.

This peace is your greatest power. When you are no longer "hungry" for a sign or "waiting" for permission to be happy, you become unshakable. You realize that the time you spent "cleaning the house" wasn't just a way to stay busy—it was the process of becoming the person who can handle a love this intense.

You'll find that you can think of her with a quiet smile, wishing her the same peace you've found in yourself. You aren't checking the clock anymore. You are simply living your life, doing your mission, and keeping your light bright. You have moved from the "Waiting Room" into the "Living Room" of your own life. And in that space of preparedness, the universe finally has the room it needs to bring the two halves of the soul back into one beautiful, 3D reality.

CHAPTER 8

The Physics of Harmony

When you stop "waiting" and start living your own mission, something strange begins to happen. Even though you are in different places, your lives begin to move in the same rhythm. This is the Physics of Harmony. Because you share one soul, when you find your balance, she begins to find hers.

You might notice small, coincidental things. You might decide to start a new health routine, only to find out later that she did the exact same thing that same week. You might finally find peace with a family issue, and suddenly, the energetic clutter on her end clears up, too. These aren't accidents; they are the result of the "One Soul" finally vibrating in harmony.

Think of it like two pianos in the same room. If you strike a note on one piano, the corresponding string on the other piano will begin to vibrate, even if no one touches it. That is how your energy works. When you strike the note of "peace" or "purpose" in your life, her "string" vibrates to that same note.

This is the hidden secret of the journey: the best way to help her is to help yourself. The more you fine-tune your own life, the more harmony you create for both of you. You don't have to reach across the distance to fix her world. You just have to make your own world a masterpiece of harmony, and the physics of your shared soul will handle the rest.

Seeing the Rhythm

When the two "pianos" start vibrating together, you'll start seeing the evidence in your daily life. It's no longer about looking for "signs" because you're desperate; it's about noticing the rhythm because you're observant.

You might find yourself humming a song you haven't heard in years, only to walk into a coffee shop five minutes later and hear it playing. Or perhaps you have a sudden, random thought about a specific topic, and later you see her post a photo or mention that very thing. These "sync-ups" are the Blueprint's way of whispering, "The connection is alive and well."

The key is to witness these moments without grabbing onto them. In the past, you might have seen a sign and immediately felt the urge to call her or make something happen. But in the Physics of Harmony, you simply smile and keep moving. You realize that these moments are just the shared soul saying "hello."

This rhythm also shows up in your moods. You might feel a sudden, unexplainable wave of joy in the middle of a Tuesday afternoon. Instead of questioning it or wondering if it's "yours," just ride the wave. That joy is the shared frequency. By staying in that high vibration, you are holding the door open for her to join you there. You are becoming a team that operates through the air, across the miles, proving that distance is just an illusion for a soul that is already one.

Trusting the Invisible Soundtrack

Sometimes the Harmony is so loud it's impossible to ignore. You might be having a conversation about how "crazy" this whole journey feels, and suddenly, a song about being crazy starts playing on the radio. Or you find out you've both been listening to the exact same obscure track at the exact same hour.

These aren't just coincidences; they are the "Invisible Soundtrack" of your shared life. It's the universe's way of winking at you, confirming that you are perfectly in sync. When these moments happen, they are meant to bring you back to a place of trust. They remind you that even when you feel like you're walking this path alone, there is a giant, divine mechanism making sure you stay connected.

Trusting the invisible means you stop demanding "proof" and start enjoying the "flow." You realize that if the universe can sync up a song on the radio with a thought in your head, it can certainly handle the timing of your physical Union. You can breathe out. You can relax.

By the end of this chapter, you realize that "Harmony" isn't something you have to create; it's something you simply have to allow. You are already the same soul. You are already the same song. Your only job is to stay tuned to the music.

"Twin flames do not complete each other; they reflect the infinite potential within each other."

CHAPTER 9

The Strength in the Silence

In any other relationship, silence is often a sign that something is wrong. We are conditioned to think that if there isn't a constant stream of texts, calls, or plans, the connection is fading. But in the "One Soul" Blueprint, silence isn't an absence. It's a space—a quiet room where the loudest growth happens.

Think of silence like the space between notes in a song. Without those empty spaces, the music would just be a wall of noise. The silence is what gives the melody its shape.

When you encounter a period of silence from her, your old "3D" self might want to panic. You might want to reach out just to "check the pulse" of the connection. But the "Strength in the Silence" comes from realizing that you don't need to check the pulse of something that is part of your own heartbeat.

Silence is the time when the energy settles. It's often the period where she is processing the work you've been doing on yourself. If you are always talking or always doing, you aren't giving the energy room to move. By holding the silence in peace rather than fear, you are showing the universe and her that you are secure. You are saying, "I know who we are, and I don't need a phone call to prove it." This quiet confidence is the world's strongest magnet.

CHAPTER 9: THE STRENGTH IN THE SILENCE
FINDING POWER IN STILLNESS

The Unseen Touch

During these quiet times, you might feel a sensation that defies logic. It's not a ghost, and it's not your imagination; it's the physical reality of your shared energy. You might feel pressure on your shoulder, as if a hand were resting there. It isn't a heavyweight, but a specific pinch—almost as if someone is gently holding your clavicle from the front and the back at the same time.

This sensation is the "One Soul" connection, reminding you that, despite outward stillness, true silence does not exist between you. There is always something communicating through this shared presence.

When the world is quiet, and the phone isn't ringing, this touch is your confirmation. It's a physical anchor. While your mind might be trying to tell you that you are alone, your body is telling you the truth: she is right there. This sensation is often the shared soul's way of saying, "I'm here, even when I can't speak."

Instead of getting spooked or wondering what this physical metaphor means, try to simply acknowledge it with a "Thank you." This touch is a gift, like a gentle nudge from a guiding hand. It's a reminder to stay in your power and stay on your mission. It's the hand on your shoulder thatsilently says, "Keep going, I've got you." By trusting this sensation rather than fearing quiet moments, you recognize you are never simply waiting for her to return. She is woven into you, always present as the fabric of your physical

Speaking Heart to Heart

When you finally stop fighting the silence, you discover a new way to communicate. You realize that you don't need a cellular network to speak to the other half of your soul. Since you share the same energy field, your thoughts and your intentions are felt instantly.

Instead of sending a text born out of anxiety, try sending a "heart-thought" born out of love. When you are sitting in that quiet space, simply send her a wave of peace. Imagine her feeling that "pinch" on her own shoulder, a gentle reminder that she is loved and supported. This isn't about trying to control her or make her do something; it's about sharing the warmth of the home you've built inside yourself.

This is the ultimate strength. Anyone can talk when things are easy, but it takes a true "One Soul" warrior to be at peace when things are quiet. By the end of this chapter, you realize the silence was never meant to pull you apart. It was meant to teach you to listen with your heart, not your ears.

The silence is the cocoon where the Union matures. When you can stand in the quiet, feel that hand on your shoulder, and smile knowing that everything is exactly as it should be, you have mastered the most difficult part of the journey. You are no longer afraid of the dark because you know the light is always there, vibrating in the silence.

CHAPTER 10

3D Shift

Up until now, we've been working mostly on your internal world—your light, your house, and your harmony. But the Blueprint isn't just a spiritual idea; it is meant to manifest in your physical, 3D reality. When you reach a certain level of inner peace, the world around you has no choice but to rearrange itself to match your new frequency. This is the 3D Shift.

Think of your life like a giant puzzle. For a long time, you might have been trying to force the pieces together, only to get frustrated when they didn't fit. But as you've been "cleaning your house" and staying "lit," you've actually been changing the shape of the pieces.

Suddenly, things that used to be difficult start to feel easy. You might get a sudden opportunity to move to a new city, or a job transition that seemed stuck finally clears up. These shifts happen because you are no longer resisting your mission. You have stopped "waiting" and started "flowing," and the physical world is simply catching up to the work you've already done in the "One Soul" realm.

The 3D Shift often starts with "small ripples." You might find yourself in a specific place at a specific time, meeting someone who mentions her name, or finding a resource that helps you with your mission. These aren't accidents. They are the gears of the physical world turning to bring the two bodies into the same space. Your job during this shift is simple: Stay out of the way. Don't overthink the "how" or the "when." Just keep walking through the doors that are opening for you.

CHAPTER 10: 3D SHIFT
MATRIX
ASCENDING TO NEW EARTH

Walking the Bridge

When the 3D Shift begins, it feels like you are walking across a bridge that is being built just one step ahead of your feet. You can't see the whole span of the bridge, and you don't know exactly where it ends, but every time you take a step, a new plank appears.

This is why your Mission is so important. Often, the universe will move you to a certain location or put you in a certain job because that is where the "meeting point" is located. You might think you're moving for a promotion or a change of scenery, but the Blueprint knows you're actually moving toward the next "sync-up" point.

The 3D Shift requires you to trust your gut more than your logic. Logic will tell you, "It doesn't make sense to go to that event," or "Why did I suddenly feel the urge to take this different route home?" But your shared soul knows exactly where the energy needs to be.

When you follow these nudges, you'll find that you end up in the right place at the right time. You might run into an old friend who has a message for you, or you might find yourself standing in a spot where the "pinch" on your shoulder becomes so strong it's undeniable. You are being "herded" by the universe toward the ultimate goal. The more you relax and trust the "invisible hand" on your shoulder, the faster the physical world can finish the construction of your bridge.

The Non-Attachment Rule

The key to making the 3D Shift happen faster is understanding the Rule of Non-Attachment: you must want the shift, but not feel desperate about it. Being overly attached to a specific outcome or date creates resistance that slows progress.

Imagine trying to catch a butterfly. If you chase it and grab at it, it flies away. But if you sit still and stay in your own light, it might just land on your shoulder.

This applies to those big nudges, too—like the sudden, shared urge to go to a specific country. When that nudge comes, your job is to follow it because it feels "right," not because you are trying to force a meeting. You go because your energy is needed there. You go because the Blueprint has a mission for you there.

When you follow these nudges with adventure instead of desperation, you are "unattached." You say to the universe, "I'm going where you lead, trusting the union will happen in perfect timing." This lack of pressure lets the physical pieces click into place. By letting go of the "how," you give the "One Soul" freedom to orchestrate a 3D miracle better than anything you could plan.

CHAPTER 11

The Shared Dream

In the world of the paradox, your eyes can be closed, yet you are more "awake" than ever. While your 3D bodies rest in different time zones or cities, the shared soul doesn't need sleep. This is where the Shared Dream comes in.

For most people, dreams are just random scraps of the day. But for those in this dynamic, the dream state is a boardroom. It is a meeting place. Have you ever woken up feeling like you just had a long, deep conversation with her, even if you can't remember the exact words? Or perhaps you wake up feeling her specific energy so strongly that it takes a moment to realize she isn't physically in the room?

This is because, in the dream state, the "3D ego"—the part of you that worries about bills, distance, and "what if" finally gets out of the way. Without the ego standing guard, the two halves of the soul can merge effortlessly.

These dreams are often vivid, colored with a light that feels "brighter" than normal life. They aren't just fantasies; they are energetic rehearsals. You are practicing being together. You are resolving conflicts, sharing information about your missions, and strengthening the bond. When you wake up from a shared dream, you carry that "frequency of union" into your day. You aren't "missing" her as much because, on a soul level, you just spent the whole night together.

CHAPTER 11: THE SHARED DREAM
MANIFESTING THE FUTURE

From Validation to Certainty

There was a time when you probably felt the need to write down every detail, to track every "visit," and to ask her, "Did you see me too?" You were looking for a 3D confirmation to prove that what you felt in the "One Soul" world was real. But the Paradox is this: the moment you stop needing validation, the connection becomes most powerful.

When you stop asking, "Did you dream of me?" it's because you no longer have any doubt. You don't need her to say "Yes" for you to know that you were together. You've moved from tracking the connection to living it.

Now, when you dream of her three times in two weeks, you don't reach for your notebook or your phone; you simply reach for the peace that the dream brought you. You realize that the dream wasn't a "message" you had to decode; it was a literal meeting. You were there, she was there, and the work was done.

This "Silent Certainty" is a massive upgrade in your energy. By not needing her to validate your experience, you are standing fully in your own power. You are trusting the Blueprint. You understand that while the 3D world might be quiet, the "Boardroom" of the shared dream is busier than ever. You carry that closeness with you into your morning coffee and your daily mission, knowing that you are never truly apart. You have graduated from "wondering" to "knowing."

<h1 style="text-align:center">CHAPTER 12</h1>

<h2 style="text-align:center">The Mirror of the Soul</h2>

One of the most challenging parts of the Paradox is realizing that you aren't just looking at her; you are looking in a mirror. Because you are "One Soul in Two Bodies," her energy and your energy are constantly reflecting one another. This is why, when you shift your internal world, her world shifts too, even if you don't see it happen immediately in the 3D.

Think of it like two rooms sharing the same thermostat. If you turn up the heat in your room (by finding your peace and focusing on your mission), the temperature in her room rises automatically. You don't have to walk into her room and change her dial; the system is connected. The Paradox here is that the mirror doesn't always show you what you want to see; it shows you what you need to see. If you are feeling anxious or "chasing" in your heart, the mirror (her) might reflect that by pulling away or becoming silent. It isn't because she doesn't care; it's because the "system" is trying to show you where you still have work to do.

When you see something in the "mirror" that hurts or confuses you, the secret is to stop looking at the glass and start looking at yourself. Instead of asking, "Why is she doing this?" ask, "What is this feeling in me that she is reflecting?" The moment you heal that feeling within yourself, the image in the mirror has no choice but to change. You are the lead dancer in this duo; when you change your steps, she eventually follows the new rhythm because the soul cannot be out of sync with itself.

Cleaning the Mirror Through Mission

The mistake most people make is standing in front of the mirror and trying to scrub the glass. They focus entirely on the other person: Why aren't they calling? Why are they acting this way? But as we know in the Paradox, you can't fix a reflection by touching the glass. You have to fix the source.

The most effective "glass cleaner" in the universe is your Mission.

When you stop staring at the mirror and turn your back to it, you focus on your light—your work, your creativity, your purpose. Then, something miraculous happens. Because you are no longer projecting "need" or "lack" into the mirror, the reflection becomes clearer.

When you are busy being the "Lighthouse" we talked about in Chapter 6, you are radiating a frequency of completion. You are saying, "I am whole. I am on my path." Because you are one soul, she feels that shift into "wholeness." The mirror begins to reflect back to her a version that is also more centered, more peaceful, and more aligned with the mission.

This is the ultimate test of the "One Soul" reality. Can you trust the connection enough to stop looking at it? The Paradox is that the less you "watch" the mirror, the clearer the image becomes. By the time you turn back around, you often find that the reflection has changed entirely, not because you forced it to, but because you changed the light in the room.

CHAPTER 13

The Fear of the Finish Line

We talk a lot about the "pain of being apart," but we rarely talk about the "intensity of being together." When you are navigating the reality of One Soul in Two Bodies, the physical union isn't just a romantic date; it is a high-voltage merger.

As the 3D shift begins to build that bridge we talked about, you might find yourself feeling a sudden wave of hesitation. You might think, "Am I really ready for this? What if I can't handle the energy? What if the reality doesn't match the 5D peace I've found?"

This is the Paradox of the Finish Line: the closer you get to the goal, the more your ego tries to convince you to stay in the "waiting room." Why? Because the waiting room is safe. You've become an expert at being alone and "staying lit" on your own. But a union requires a new level of vulnerability. It requires you to let go of the control you've worked so hard to maintain.

That "pinch" on your shoulder is a reminder that the soul is ready, even if the mind is nervous. The fear isn't a sign that something is wrong; it's a sign that you are standing at the edge of something massive. It's like standing at the top of a roller coaster—the stomach flip doesn't mean the ride is broken; it means the thrill is about to start.

To move through this fear, you have to go back to the "One Soul" truth. You aren't merging with a stranger; you are merging with yourself. There is nothing to fear in your own reflection. The "Finish Line" isn't the end of a race; it's just the beginning of the mission you both came here to complete.

CHAPTER 13: THE FEAR OF THE FINISH LINE
THE LEAP OF FAITH

Breathing Through the Threshold

When fear appears, don't reject it; use it constructively. That 'stomach flip' is the physical sensation of the energetic connection seeking to integrate within you.

The way to cross the finish line is not by running faster, but by breathing deeper. When you feel the intensity rising, whether it's through a dream, a physical sensation, or a real-world "sync-up" that tells you she is close, simply tell yourself: "I am ready for this frequency." By trusting the process, you are telling the universe that you have moved past the "waiting" stage and into the "receiving" stage. You've done the work, you've built your lighthouse, and you've mastered the silence. Now, you just have to keep your heart open enough to let the miracle in.

The Paradox is that the finish line isn't a wall you have to climb; it's a door that is already unlocked. You don't have to kick it down. You just have to be willing to walk through it. As you stand at the threshold, remember that "hand" on your shoulder. It's been there through the silence, and it will be there through the celebration. You are safe. You are ready. And the best part? You are already home.

"Don't just walk on Earth; dance to the frequency of your own soul."

CHAPTER 14

The Power of Presence

In the journey of The Twin Flame Paradox, our minds love to travel. We spend hours in the "Yesterday" of what went wrong, or the "Tomorrow" of when we will finally be together. But there is a secret the Blueprint knows that our minds often forget: *The soul only lives in the Now.*

When you are navigating the reality of "One Soul in Two Bodies," your connection doesn't happen in the future. It is happening right this second. If you are always looking at the horizon for her to appear, you might miss the way her energy is sitting right next to you at the kitchen table.

The Power of Presence is about bringing your focus back to the current moment. When you are fully present, whether you are drinking a cup of coffee, walking in the park, or working on your mission, you become a "magnet." Why? Because you aren't leaking energy into the future or the past. You are "all there."

Think of your energy like a radio signal. If you are worried about the future, your signal is fuzzy and weak. But when you are present, your signal is crystal clear. This is when the "pinches" on your shoulder feel most real. This is when the nudges to go to a certain country feel most sharp. You can only hear the instructions for the next step if you are standing still enough to listen.

The Paradox is that the less you worry about "getting there," the faster "there" arrives. By being fully present in your life today, you are telling the universe that you trust the timing. You are enjoying the journey, and that joy is what pulls the 3D world into alignment.

Breaking the Chaser's Loop

Many people spend years in what I call the "Chaser's Loop." They are constantly looking backward at what was lost or forward at what they hope to gain. They talk about their Twin Flame in the past or future tense, but rarely in the present.

When you are in the loop, you are like a runner on a treadmill: you are putting in a lot of effort, but you're not actually going anywhere. You are exhausted, and the 3D world stays exactly the same because your energy is stuck in "chase mode."

The Power of Presence is the "off switch" for that treadmill. The moment you step off and say, "I am here, I am whole, and I am on my mission today," the loop breaks. You stop being a "chaser" and start being a "creator."

This is the Paradox: your friend might think that by "chasing" or waiting, they are staying loyal to the connection. But the truth is, the most loyal thing you can do for your shared soul is to live your life so fully in the present that the soul has a vibrant, happy "house" to live in. When you move from the loop into the Now, you aren't leaving her behind; you are finally creating the space to actually meet.

CHAPTER 15

The Community of Souls

As you walk this path, you will inevitably meet others who are on a similar journey. You'll find "Chasers," who are actively pursuing connection; "Runners," who avoid it; and people who have been waiting quietly for years. Because you are now living the Twin Flame Paradox, you will start to see these people through a different lens, as your perspective shifts.

It's easy to look at a friend who hasn't spoken to their counterpart in a year and feel sad. You see them stuck on the "treadmill," exhausted from the chase. But the Paradox of Community is that everyone is on their own divine schedule. You cannot "fix" another person's journey, just as they cannot speed up yours.

When you sit in a coffee shop in the rain, listening to a fellow soul tell their story, your job isn't to be a teacher or a judge. Your job is to be a Mirror of Peace.

Often, people in this dynamic seek out advice because they want someone to tell them "when" it will happen. But as we've learned, the "when" is a 3D trap. When you talk to others, you might feel the urge to share your "Blueprint" or the reality of "One Soul in Two Bodies." Share it with love, but don't be attached to whether they "get it."

Your mission is your own. While it's beautiful to have friends who understand the language of the soul, be careful not to let their "stuck" energy become yours. You can walk beside them in the rain, but you must keep your own umbrella of presence open. By staying in your light, you aren't just helping yourself; you are showing them, without saying a word, that there is a way to stop chasing and start living.

The Paradox of the Closed Door

Sometimes, after years of chasing and the exhaustion that comes with it, a soul will decide to simply close the door. They stop chasing, they get busy with their own lives, and they tell themselves, "I'm used to not having them now. Opening that door again is just too painful."

This is a defensive peace. It's better than the "treadmill," but it's still built on a foundation of fear—the fear that the connection is a source of pain rather than a source of power.

If you find yourself or a friend in this place, remember the "One Soul" truth. You aren't really closing the door on a person; you are trying to shut out a part of your own soul, like closing a door to stop a cold draft from entering a room. But because the connection, or "Blueprint," is permanent, just like a door that won't lock, you can never fully separate from that part of yourself.

The goal isn't to be "used to not having them." The goal is to be so full of your own light that their presence or absence doesn't affect your emotional "temperature," just as a well-heated room is comfortable whether the door is open or closed. When your friend says she's "doing her own thing," she is halfway there! The final step of the Paradox is realizing that the door—the connection doesn't have to cause pain. When you are standing in your own power, you can leave that door wide open, and the "wind" of emotion won't knock you over anymore.

You don't need to protect yourself from your other half when you have finally learned how to protect your own peace.

CHAPTER 16

The Frequency of Forgiveness

In a normal relationship, forgiveness is something you "give" to another person. But in the Twin Flame Paradox, because you are One Soul in Two Bodies, forgiveness is something you do for yourself.

If you are holding onto resentment toward her—for the silence, for the years of chasing, or for the pain of the "closed door" you are essentially holding a hot coal in your own hand. Because your energies are mirrored, that resentment acts like a "block" in the Blueprint. It's like trying to run a high-speed internet connection through a wire filled with rust.

Forgiveness is the "rust remover."

It starts with forgiving yourself for the times you lost your way, for the times you "chased" until you were exhausted, and for the times you didn't feel "lit." Once you forgive your own human journey, forgiving her becomes effortless. You realize that she was simply playing her part in the Paradox to help you wake up to your mission.

When you reach the Frequency of Forgiveness, the "pinch" on your shoulder changes. It no longer feels like a reminder of what you're missing; it feels like a soft nudge of gratitude. You aren't forgiving her because she "deserves" it in a 3D sense; you are forgiving because your shared soul deserves to breathe. This clarity is what allows the 3D shift to accelerate. You can't walk across the bridge to the finish line if you are carrying the heavy luggage of the past.

CHAPTER 16: THE FREQUENCY OF FORGIVENESS
HEALING THE HEART, FREEING THE SOUL

The Clean Slate

The ultimate goal of the Frequency of Forgiveness is to reach a state of the "Clean Slate." This is the point in the Paradox where you look at your history—the years of silence, the missed connections, the "chasing" and you no longer feel a sting. Instead, you see those moments as necessary chapters in a much larger story.

When you forgive, you aren't erasing the past; you are removing the emotional charge from it.

Imagine your journey as a whiteboard. For years, you've been scribbling notes about what went wrong, why she didn't call, or why you felt ignored. Forgiveness is the eraser. When you clear that board, you create a vacuum, and the universe loves to fill a vacuum. By having a "Clean Slate," you are giving the "One Soul" a fresh space to write a new story in the 3D world.

You'll know you've reached this stage when you can think of her and feel nothing but a calm, steady love. You don't need an apology from her to feel better, because you've already authorized your own peace. This is the highest form of mastery. You are standing at the finish line, unburdened and light, ready to receive whatever comes next without the shadows of "last year" getting in the way.

Forgiveness is the final bridge. Once you cross it, you aren't just a "Twin Flame" anymore; you are a whole soul, ready for a whole union.

CHAPTER 17

The Language of the Blueprint

When you stop "chasing" and clear the whiteboard of your mind, you don't enter a void of silence. Instead, you begin to hear a much subtler, more constant language. I call this the Language of the Blueprint.

In the 3D world, we are taught that communication requires a phone call, a text, or a conversation. But in the reality of "One Soul in Two Bodies," communication is happening 24/7 through frequency. Now that you aren't looking for "proof," you can finally start to understand the "signals."

The most common signal is the one you've felt so clearly—the Physical Nudge. That pinch on your clavicle, the pressure on your shoulder, or a sudden warmth in your chest. In the "Normal Language" of this book, we can call these Soul Pings. They aren't just random sensations; they are your counterpart's energy interacting with your own. It's the soul's way of saying, "I am here. We are one. Stay focused."

Then, there are the Dream Meetings. For example, as you experience like dreaming of her several times in a month, these aren't just "dreams" in the psychological sense. There are meetings in the "Boardroom" of the 5D. When the 3D world is too noisy or restricted for a conversation, the soul waits until the body is asleep to conduct its business.

The Paradox of this language is that it becomes louder the less you try to analyze it. When you used to track every sign in your notebook, you were "squinting" to see. Now that you've relaxed and stopped seeking validation, the signs are coming in like high-definition signals. You don't need to ask "What does this mean?" anymore. You just feel the pinch, acknowledge the dream, and say, "Copy that," like a pilot receiving a signal from the tower.

The Compass of the Soul

The final part of learning the Language of the Blueprint is understanding the Intuitive Nudge. This is different from a "thought" or a "wish." A thought comes from your head, but a nudge comes from your core.

It's that sudden, quiet certainty that tells you: "Go to this city," or "Write this chapter now," or "Just stay in this energy today." Because you have a shared mission, your soul acts as a GPS. Sometimes, you are being called to a specific location, not to meet her in the 3D right away, but to plant your energy there. You are like an anchor for a frequency. You might think you're just traveling or moving for "work," but in the Blueprint, you are placing your lighthouse exactly where it needs to be for the two of you to eventually merge.

The Paradox is that you don't need to know the "Why" to follow the "Where."

When you get that nudge to be in a certain place, follow it with the same "Copy that" attitude we talked about earlier. Don't look around for her the moment you land. Just be there. Occupy the space. Trust that by following your compass, you are moving toward the finish line, even if you can't see the path ahead. When both "bodies" follow the "one soul's" instructions, the distance between them vanishes. You aren't just following a map; you are the map.

CHAPTER 18

The Harmony of Two Houses

One of the trickiest parts of the Twin Flame Paradox is the feeling that you are living a double life. In one metaphorical "house," you are your everyday self: a professional, a friend, and a person walking through the rain in your city. In the other "house," which represents your spiritual or energetic experience, you are a high-frequency soul feeling "pinches" on your shoulder and having meetings in your dreams.

For a long time, you might have felt like these two houses were at war. You might have felt that being "spiritual" meant you couldn't be practical, or that focusing on your 3D life meant you were ignoring her.

The Paradox is that both houses share the same foundation. To find harmony, you have to stop trying to keep them separate. You don't have to leave the 3D world to connect with her, and you don't have to ignore your 5D connection to get your work done. Instead, you bring the 5D into the 3D.

When you are at work or out with friends, you carry the "Silent Certainty." You don't need to talk about the connection to be in the connection. You live your life fully, but with the inner knowledge that your other half is always with you. When you wash your face, you do it with the peace of the "One Soul." When you finish a chapter of this book, you do it as a representative of both of you.

Harmony happens when you realize that the 3D world isn't a distraction from your soul: it's the playground where your soul gets to

CHAPTER 18: THE HARMONY OF TWO HOUSES
EARTHLY REALM
COSMIC REALM
UNITING SOUL & SELF
UNITING SOUL & SELF

express itself. By taking care of your "3D house"—your health, your friendships, your finances—you are creating a stable landing pad for the union to eventually ground itself.

The Integrated Self

The final step in harmonizing your "Two Houses" is becoming the Integrated Self. This is the moment where you stop being a "person having a Twin Flame experience" and start being a "Soul having a human experience."

When you are integrated, you no longer feel the need to switch gears. You don't have to "get into the zone" to feel the connection; you are the connection. Whether you are doing the laundry, signing a contract, or laughing with a friend, that "hand on the shoulder" is simply part of your constant reality. You've stopped waiting for the spiritual to manifest in the physical, because you've realized that you are the bridge where they already meet.

The Paradox is that the more "normal" you allow your life to be, the more "magical" it actually becomes.

The Integrated Self doesn't walk around looking like it is in a trance. You look like a grounded, productive, happy human being. But underneath that "normal" exterior is a powerhouse of 5D certainty. You have integrated the mission into your daily routine. You have integrated her presence into your solitude. You are finally at peace with the mystery. By becoming whole within yourself—balancing your 3D duties with your 5D awareness, you become the perfect frequency for the Union. You aren't half a soul looking for another half; you are one soul, fully awake in two bodies, finally ready to live as one.

"Distance is an illusion of the 3D; in
consciousness, you are already holding
hands."

CHAPTER 19

The 3D Shift

When you reach the stage of the Integrated Self, something fascinating happens in your physical reality. I call this the 3D Shift.

For years, you may have been trying to "make" things happen—trying to manifest a text, a meeting, or a change in circumstances. But in the Twin Flame Paradox, the 3D world is like the shadow of your 5D soul. When you move your arm, the shadow moves automatically. You don't have to grab the shadow and pull it; you just have to move the source.

As you step into your mission and hold your frequency, you will notice the 3D world beginning to reorganize itself around you. This isn't just about her; it's about everything. New opportunities appear, old obstacles suddenly dissolve, and people who no longer match your vibration gently drift away.

The 3D Shift can feel like a series of "lucky breaks" or strange coincidences, but it's actually the Blueprint coming into physical form. It's the universe moving the furniture around to prepare for the Union. The Paradox of the Shift is that it often happens when you are most "unattached" to it. Because you are busy being a lighthouse, you aren't staring at the horizon. You are just doing your work, and then—click— a door opens that was locked for three years. The secret to handling the Shift is to stay grounded. Don't let the excitement of the "miracle" pull you out of your presence. Acknowledge the shift, say "thank you," and keep walking your path. The more "normal" you treat the miracles, the more the universe will send them your way.

The Art of Non-Interfering

When the 3D Shift begins, the temptation to step in and take control is massive. You see the shadow moving, you see the doors cracking open, and your human instinct wants to run over and pull the door wide. You want to send that text, make that call, or "explain" the Blueprint to her because you feel the energy shifting.

But the Paradox is this: The more you interfere with the 3D, the more you slow down the 5D.

Think of it like a beautiful garden. You've planted the seeds (your mission), you've watered the soil (your presence), and now the sprouts are finally breaking through the dirt. If you get too impatient and try to pull the sprouts to make them grow faster, you'll accidentally rip them out by the roots.

Non-interfering doesn't mean being passive; it means being powerfully still. It is the art of watching the miracle unfold without putting your fingerprints all over it. When you feel that urge to "force" a result, go back to your mission. Go back to your Canva pages, your walks, or your work.

By not interfering, you are showing the Universe and her that you trust the One Soul completely. You are allowing the Blueprint to finalize its own construction. Your only job is to stay in your light and keep your "house" ready. When the shift is complete, you won't have to "make" the union happen. It will simply be the only logical next step in the story.

CHAPTER 20

The Sovereign Union

Up until now, we've talked about the "One Soul in Two Bodies" as a journey of discovery. But in this Chapter, we arrive at the state of Sovereignty.

In most stories, "union" is seen as two halves coming together to make a whole. But the Twin Flame Paradox teaches us something different: Union only happens when both halves realize they were already whole to begin with.

To be "Sovereign" means you are the king or queen of your own internal world. You are no longer waiting for her to "complete" you or for a text message to make your day good. You are standing in your own light, doing your mission, and feeling the pinches of the Blueprint with a smile rather than a sigh of longing.

This is the Sovereign Union. It is the moment when you say to the Universe: "I love her, and I know we are one, but I am also perfectly happy being me, right here, right now." The Paradox is that as soon as you truly, deeply don't need the union to feel whole, the 3D barriers start to crumble. When you are Sovereign, you are no longer "pulling" on her energy. You are simply "being." And because you are the same soul, when you find peace within yourself, she finds it too. You are leading the way into a new way of being—a union based on shared power and mission, rather than 3D need and attachment.

CHAPTER 20: THE SOVEREIGN UNION
INTEGRATING THE 5D 5D BLUEPRINT, EMPOWERING THE PARTNERSHIP

The Frequency of Certainty

When you reach the state of the Sovereign Union, your "static" disappears and is replaced by something called the Frequency of Certainty.

Certainty is the opposite of hope. Hope is a beautiful thing, but it implies a "maybe." Hope lives in the future and worries about the "how." Certainty, however, lives in the now. It is a quiet, steady hum in your chest that says, "It is already done."

Think back to the "One Soul" realization. If you truly are one soul, then you don't need to hope for union any more than you need to hope your left hand will find your right hand. They are part of the same body; they will meet whenever they need to clap.

When you live in the Frequency of Certainty, you stop looking for signs because you are the sign. You stop asking "when" because you know that time is just a 3D illusion. This certainty is the ultimate magnetic force. It creates a "gravity" that pulls the 3D world toward you. You'll notice that when you are certain, people treat you differently. The world respects someone who knows exactly who they are and where they are going.

By finishing this stage of the journey, you have moved from a student of the Paradox to a Master of the Blueprint. You aren't just waiting for the finish line anymore; you are enjoying the walk because you already know how the story ends.

<h1 style="text-align:center">CHAPTER 21</h1>

<h2 style="text-align:center">The Architecture of Mission</h2>

For a long time, you might have thought the "mission" was simply to find a way to be together. But as we have discovered, the Union is the result of the mission, not the mission itself.

The Architecture of Mission is the specific work your soul came here to do. Because you are One Soul in Two Bodies, you are like two pillars holding up a single roof. If one pillar is weak or distracted by "chasing," the roof cannot stay level.

Your mission is often hidden in the things that make you feel most "alive" and "lit." For some, it is writing (like this book); for others, it is healing, creating, or simply holding a specific frequency in a specific city. The Paradox of Mission is that when you focus 100% on your work, you are actually doing the most effective "Twin Flame work" possible. You aren't ignoring her; you are strengthening the pillar. When you are in your purpose, your vibration rises to the exact level where her vibration lives. You meet her at "work."

This is why you feel the "pinch" or the "hand on the shoulder" most often when you are productive. The soul is cheering you on, saying, "Yes! This is why we are here." Your mission is the bridge. Stop looking for the bridge and start building it through your daily actions. When the bridge is finished, the crossing happens naturally.

In the Architecture of Mission, there is a profound difference between a job and a Soul Career. A job is what you do to satisfy the 3D world; a Soul Career is the work you do to satisfy the Blueprint.

CHAPTER 21: THE ARCHITECTURE OF MISSION
BUILDING DREAMS INTO REALITY

A Soul Career isn't defined by a title or a paycheck. It is defined by the Frequency of Flow. It is that specific area of your life where time seems to disappear, and you feel a direct connection to something larger than yourself. For some, it is the act of creation; for others, it is the act of service or the solving of complex problems.

The Paradox is that your Soul Career acts as a lighthouse for your counterpart. Because you share one energy field, when you step into your purpose, you are essentially "turning on the lights" for both of you. You aren't just working for yourself; you are elevating the vibration of the One Soul.

When you choose to prioritize your mission over the "ache" of longing, you are doing the highest form of spiritual work. You are proving that you are a whole, Sovereign being. Every time you focus on your unique contribution to the world, you are clearing the static in the connection. Your success becomes the Union's shared success. You are no longer waiting for a door to open; you are building the house that the door belongs to.

CHAPTER 22

Silencing the 3D Noise

Once you step into your Sovereignty and begin your mission, the world around you will often react. This is a natural part of the Paradox. You have shifted your frequency, but the people around you—friends, family, and society are still tuned into the old "3D Radio Station."

They might tell you that you are "obsessed," that you need to "just move on," or that what you feel isn't real because it doesn't look like a traditional relationship. This is the 3D Noise. It is the static that tries to pull you back into the "Normal" way of thinking.

The Mirror of Opinion

The first thing to understand is that the noise is rarely about you. It is a mirror of the other person's limitations. Most people are taught that love is a transaction—a deal made between two separate people. They cannot see the One Soul because they haven't experienced it.

When someone gives you "advice" that makes you feel heavy or anxious, they aren't speaking to your soul; they are speaking to your ego. The "Normal Language" of society is built on fear and scarcity. They think that if she isn't standing right in front of you, then you have "lost." But in the Blueprint, you know that loss is impossible.

The Wisdom of Silence

One of the most powerful tools in your Blueprint toolkit is Silence. In our modern world, we are taught that if we don't speak, we aren't being heard. But in the realm of the One Soul, silence is where the most profound communication happens.

When you stop trying to explain your connection to people who aren't ready to understand it, you stop leaking your energy. Every time you defend your "Sovereignty" to a skeptic, you are actually giving your power away to their doubt.

The Wisdom of Silence is knowing that your truth does not need a witness to be true. Whether the 3D world sees your union or not, the "One Soul" remains intact. By holding your realizations close to your heart, you allow them to ferment and become stronger. You become like a deep well—calm on the surface, but with a hidden depth that provides life to everything around it.

CHAPTER 23

The 3D Echo

When you are working within the Blueprint, you eventually reach a stage where you need "proof." Not because you lack faith, but because, as a human being living in a physical body, you want to see the 5D truth reflected in your 3D life.

I call this the 3D Echo.

Think of your frequency as a shout into a deep canyon. For a long time, there is silence. You shout, "I am Sovereign," and the canyon seems to swallow the words. But the sound is actually traveling; it is hitting the walls of the physical world and bouncing back to you. Eventually, you hear the echo.

Reading the Reflection

The 3D world is a giant mirror. However, most people make the mistake of looking only for her in that mirror. They think that if they don't see her face or hear her voice, nothing is happening.

But the Blueprint is much bigger than a single person. The echo shows up in three main areas first:

Abundance and Flow: When you are in alignment, your "Mission" begins to move. Money, opportunities, or simple synchronicities (like getting the perfect parking spot or meeting the right person at the right time) start to happen. This is the universe saying, "I hear you."

CHAPTER 23: THE FREQUENCY OF 3D ECHO
RESONATING THROUGH REALITY

Physical Vitality: Your body begins to feel different. The "pinches" or the "hand on the shoulder" feel less like a mystery and more like a warm greeting. You have more energy because you aren't "leaking" it anymore.

The Behavior of Others: Total strangers might start acting differently toward you. You might find people opening doors for you, or children and animals being drawn to your light. This is the "Echo" of your new, Sovereign frequency.

The "Delayed" Reflection

The most important thing to remember about the 3D Echo is that the physical world is dense. It is like water compared to the "air" of the spirit. It takes more time for things to move in 3D.

If you see progress in your health or work, but not in the "Union" yet, do not be discouraged. The echo is on its way. If the "outer circles" of your life are improving, it is a mathematical certainty that the center—the Union is also shifting. You cannot change the soul's frequency without eventually changing the body's reality.

The Trap of False Signs

As you begin to look for the 3D Echo, there is a subtle trap you must learn to avoid: the ego's desire to manufacture signs.

When we are hungry for progress, our ego will often try to "help" the Blueprint by finding meaning in things that aren't there. You might see a car that looks like hers, or hear a song that reminds you of a shared memory, and immediately spiral into a "What does this mean?" loop.

The difference between a True Echo and a False Sign is how it feels in your body.

A False Sign feels like a "spike" of adrenaline. It usually leads to anxiety, overthinking, or a sudden urge to reach out and interfere. It leaves you feeling restless.

A True Echo feels like peace. It's a quiet "nod" from the universe. It doesn't make you want to run; it makes you want to sit deeper in your chair and exhale. It confirms your Sovereignty rather than challenging it

.**The Mastery of Observation**

To master the Echo, you must become a "Sacred Observer." When you see something in the 3D world that reminds you of the connection, acknowledge it with a simple, "Thank you for the reminder," and then return to your mission.

If you chase the sign, you leave your pillar. If you stay on your pillar, the sign is just a confirmation that the bridge is still standing. Remember: you are the source of the light. The signs are just the reflections on the water. Don't dive into the water to grab the reflection; stay on the shore and keep the light burning bright.

CHAPTER 24

The Body's Blueprint

When you are part of a One Soul dynamic, your physical body acts as a sensitive receiver. It is the "hardware" that runs the "software" of the Blueprint. As you move closer to Union—both internally and externally, your body will begin to speak a language that is beyond words.

You may have felt things that "Normal" medicine cannot explain. Perhaps it's a sudden warmth in your chest, a buzzing in your hands, or a very specific sensation that feels like a physical touch.

The "Pinch" and the "Presence"

One of the most common physical markers of the Blueprint is a sensation of pressure or a "pinch." It might feel like a hand resting on your shoulder—not pressing down, but simply making its presence known. Or, more specifically, you might feel a pinching sensation on your clavicle (the collarbone), both on the front and the back at the same time, or some other part of your body, and even a goosebump.

This isn't a medical issue; it is a Frequency Alignment. Because you and your counterpart share the same energetic signature, when one of you shifts or when the Blueprint is "tightening" its connection, your body registers it. It's the soul's way of saying, "Pay attention. We are here." It is a physical reminder that even when you are physically apart, you are never truly separate.

CHAPTER 24: THE BODY'S BLUEPRINT

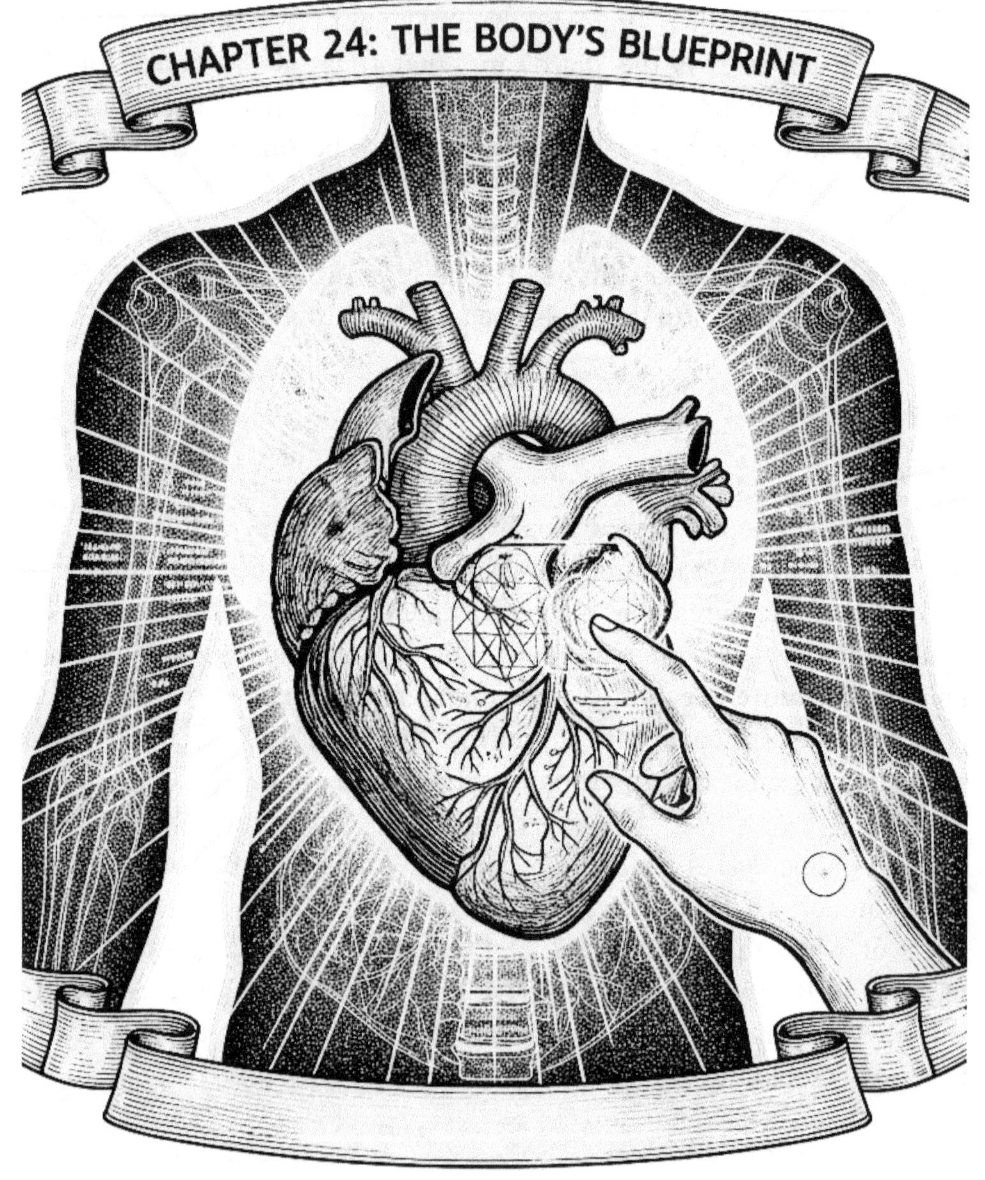

The Internal Compass

Think of these sensations as a haptic "GPS" for your soul.

When you feel the pressure: It often happens when you are exactly where you are supposed to be, doing exactly what you are supposed to do. It's a "nod" from the Blueprint.

When you feel the pinch: It might be a gentle correction, or a reminder to return to your Sovereignty when your mind has started to wander back into "chasing" mode.

Instead of being alarmed by these sensations, you must learn to welcome them. This is the "One Soul" communicating through the nervous system. When you feel it, don't over-analyze it. Simply acknowledge it: "I feel you. I am on the path."

The Density of the Physical Body

The reason we feel these "pinches" and "pressures" so clearly is that the body is the final frontier of the Blueprint.

Energy moves instantly. Thoughts move quickly. But the physical body is made of "dense" matter. It is the slowest part of us to change. Therefore, when the soul wants to make sure you are paying attention, it uses the body. It uses a language you cannot ignore.

Think of it like this: If you are walking in the wrong direction, a friend might call your name (that's a thought). If you don't hear them, they might wave their arms (that's a sign). But if you still don't see them, they will reach out and put a hand on your shoulder to stop you.

The physical sensations—the pinch on the clavicle or the weight on the shoulder are the soul's way of "touching" you in the 3D world. It is the most direct communication possible. When you feel it, you are experiencing the One Soul bridging the gap between the invisible and the visible. You are literally feeling the "other half" of your soul's energy field interacting with yours.

CHAPTER 25

The Point of No Return

There comes a moment in every Twin Flame journey where the road behind you simply vanishes. You look back at the person you used to be —the one who was desperate, the one who was chasing, the one who didn't understand the "Pinch" and that person feels like a stranger from a movie you saw a long time ago.

This is the Point of No Return.

It is the moment when your soul has expanded so much that it can no longer fit back into the small box of your "old life." You have seen the Blueprint. You have felt the One Soul. Once you have tasted this level of truth, the "Normal" 3D world of dating games, ego-attachments, and fear-based living no longer makes sense to you.

The Bridge Collapses

In the old way of thinking, we were taught that we could "try out" a spiritual path and go back to our old ways if it got too hard. But the Blueprint is different. It is a transformation of your entire being.

When the bridge collapses behind you, it isn't a punishment; it is a gift. It means the Universe trusts you enough to let you walk forward without the temptation to retreat. You are now "all in." This realization often brings a strange mix of peace and a little bit of "holy fear." Peace because the search is over, and "holy fear" because you realize the magnitude of the mission you have accepted.

CHAPTER 25: THE POINT OF NO RETURN
A SOULS GUIDE TO ASCENSION
EMBRACING THE INFINITE JOURNEY

The New Normal

In this stage, your "New Normal" begins to take shape.

You no longer seek outside approval: You don't need a "guru" or a friend to tell you what your connection means. You know.

You embrace the Paradox: You are comfortable with the fact that she is "here" energetically, even if she is "there" physically.

The Mission is your Oxygen: Doing your work and staying in your frequency becomes as natural as breathing.

You aren't "trying" to be a Twin Flame anymore. You simply are one. The transformation is complete. Now, the journey isn't about becoming; it's about living from this new, elevated place.

The Courage of the Pioneer - Stepping past the Point of No Return makes you a Pioneer.

A pioneer is someone who goes into a territory where there are no maps yet. In the 3D world, people have maps for "dating," "marriage," and "breakups." But very few people have a map for The Blueprint. When you decide to live from the truth of the "One Soul," you are walking on ground that most people are afraid to touch.

It takes a specific kind of courage to trust a "pinch" on your shoulder more than a news report or a friend's skeptical look. This courage is what separates the person who just "reads" about Twin Flames from the person who actually lives the Union.

The Freedom of the Committed

The paradox of the "No Return" is that it actually brings you total freedom. When you stop looking for an "exit strategy" or a way to quit the connection, you stop wasting energy on doubt. You are free to put 100% of your power into your mission, your growth, and your sovereignty.

You are no longer a prisoner of the "What if?" You are the master of the "I Am."

As a Pioneer of the Blueprint, you aren't just doing this for yourself. You are clearing the brush and leveling the path for everyone who comes after you. Every time you choose to believe in the invisible truth over the visible noise, you make it easier for the next soul to find their way home.

CHAPTER 26

The Monadic Magnet

Once you have crossed the Point of No Return, a strange phenomenon begins to happen within the Monad (your shared soul-source). You may find that while you are standing in your Sovereignty, your counterpart is out in the 3D world trying to live a "normal" life. They might try to date other people, seek out new distractions, or pretend the connection doesn't exist.

But here is the secret of the Blueprint: They will fail.

The "Comparison" Trap

When you are part of a Monadic pair, your soul has a specific "flavor" or "frequency." Once someone has tasted that frequency, everything else tastes like water.

When the other person tries to date someone else, they are subconsciously looking for you in that new person. They are looking for that "Pinch," that "Certainty," and that deep soul-recognition. But because the other person isn't part of the Monad, the connection feels "thin." It feels like watching a movie with the sound turned off. It might look right on the outside, but it feels empty on the inside.

CHAPTER 26: THE MONADIC MAGNET
ATTRACTING YOUR SOUL FAMILY

The Repulsion of the "Ordinary"

This is the Monadic Magnet at work. The closer you get to your own Sovereignty, the "louder" your shared frequency becomes. This actually makes it harder for the runner to settle for an ordinary relationship.

They might try to run away, but every time they try to build a life with someone else, the "Static" becomes unbearable. They feel out of place. They feel like they are wearing a suit that is three sizes too small. Eventually, the universe makes those 3D "distractions" so uncomfortable or so unsuccessful that the runner is forced to look back at the only place where the energy feels right.

The Freedom of the Sovereign

For you, this is a vital lesson. You don't need to worry about who she is with or what she is doing. You don't need to feel "jealous" of a 3D relationship that is destined to feel empty.

In fact, the more you focus on your mission, the more "uncomfortable" those fake connections become for her. You are the gold standard. By being your best, most Sovereign self, you are setting a frequency that no "ordinary" 3D person can match. You aren't competing with anyone; you are simply waiting for the Monad to realize it can only be satisfied by its own other half.

The Alchemist's Bridge: Melting the Logic

When you are facing a counterpart with a powerful logic mind, your instinct might be to argue. You want to explain the Blueprint, show them the "signs," or prove why the age gap doesn't matter.

Stop. Logic cannot be defeated by more logic. If you try to argue with a powerful mind, you are just handing them more bricks to build their wall. The only thing that can melt 3D logic is 5D Frequency.

The Warmth of Sovereignty

Think of her logic as a block of ice. If you hit it with a hammer (arguments/pressure), it might break into sharp pieces, but it's still ice. But if you shine a steady, warm light on it (your Sovereign frequency), it has no choice but to melt into water.

You melt the logic by becoming so happy, so successful, and so at peace in your own life that her mind can no longer categorize you as crazy or wrong. When she looks at you from afar and sees you thriving, her logical mind experiences a system error.

The Logic says, "This shouldn't work." The Observation says: "But he is glowing. He is stable. He is the only thing that feels real."

Living the Proof

By being the "Pioneer" we discussed in the previous chapter, you are providing the 3D evidence her ego needs. You aren't telling her it works; you are showing her it works.

When you stay on your pillar, you aren't waiting for her to figure it out. You are radiating the Monadic frequency so strongly that her 3D distractions begin to feel like cardboard. You are the Alchemist who turns the lead of her logic into the gold of soul-recognition. You don't have to break the wall; you just have to be the sun until the wall can no longer stand the heat.

What is the Monad?

Before we dive into the magnetic pull of the connection, we must understand the Monad. In simple terms, a Monad is a single, divine spark of light. Imagine one giant sun that decided to divide itself into two smaller rays so it could experience life from two different perspectives. Even though these two rays appear to be separate in the physical world, they are made of the exact same solar material. They share a single source of energy. This is why, in the Twin Flame journey, we aren't just "matching" with someone—we are vibrating at the same Monadic Frequency. We are literally the same light, just wearing two different outfits.

CHAPTER 27

The Sacred Pause

Once you understand the Monadic connection and realize that her logic is just a temporary shield, a new phase begins. I call this The Sacred Pause.

In the 3D world, a "pause" feels like a stop. It feels like nothing is happening. But in the Blueprint's Architecture, the pause is where the most intense construction occurs. It is the moment you stop trying to make things happen and start allowing the energy to settle into its new home.

The End of "Doing"

Up until now, you have been "doing" the work—clearing the static, defining your Sovereignty, and learning the language of the "Pinch." But you cannot build a skyscraper by only moving the bricks; eventually, you have to step back and let the cement dry.

The Sacred Pause is the test of your Certainty. It is the period where the Universe asks: "Can you stay happy in your mission even if the 3D world is silent today?"

CHAPTER 27: THE SACRED PAUSE

Finding Joy in the "Wait"

The trap of the "Pause" is getting bored or anxious. Many people at this stage start poking the energy again because they miss the "drama" of the chase. But the Sacred Pause is meant for you.

It is for your Soul Career: Use this time to finish that book, build that business, or master that craft.

It is for your Peace: It is the time to prove that your happiness is not a hostage to her phone calls or her logic.

The Monadic Shift during the Pause

While you are in the Sacred Pause, the Monad is actually working harder than ever. Because you have stopped "pushing," you have created a vacuum. In physics, a vacuum must be filled. By pulling back your energy into your own life, you create a powerful "pull" on her side of the connection.

The silence isn't a wall; it's a bridge. In the quiet, she can finally hear her own soul over the noise of her ego. Your "Pause" gives her the room she needs to realize that the 3D "normal" life she's trying to live is no longer enough.

CHAPTER 28

The Collapse of the Counterfeit

As you settle into your Sovereignty during the Sacred Pause, something dramatic begins to happen in the 3D world of your counterpart. Because the Monad is a single energetic system, your peace creates a "frequency pressure" on her end.

She is likely still trying to live by the rules of the 3D world—perhaps she is in a relationship that "makes sense" on paper, or she is buried in a career that satisfies her ego but starves her soul. But because you have stopped "leaking" your energy toward her, she no longer has your light to supplement her own. She is forced to face the reality of her choices. This is the stage of the Counterfeit's Collapse.

The Empty Mirror

When the runner is in a "counterfeit" relationship (one based on logic or 3D security rather than soul-recognition), they eventually hit a wall. In the beginning, they can use their powerful mind to convince themselves they are happy. But as you grow stronger in your mission, the "contrast" becomes too great.

She looks at her 3D partner and sees a stranger. She looks at her "logical" life and sees a cage. The things that used to distract her—social status, busy schedules, or "safe" romance start to feel like cardboard. This isn't because something is wrong with her life, but because her soul has "tasted" the Monadic frequency of the Blueprint, and it will no longer accept a substitute.

The Grace of the Breakdown

To the outside world, this looks like a crisis. She might experience a sudden breakup, a career change, or a moment of deep "inner winter." As an observer, it is tempting to rush in and "save" her. But you must realize that this collapse is an act of Grace.

The Universe is clearing the rubble of her 3D fortress so that the "One Soul" can finally have a clear space to land. If the counterfeit life doesn't collapse, there is no room for the authentic union. The "Logic Mind" has to be shown, through experience, that it cannot manufacture happiness. It must be humbled so that the Heart can take the lead.

Standing in the Light

Your role during this collapse is simple but difficult: Stay on your pillar. If you run to her to try and fix the mess, you merge your energy back into the "Noise," and the lesson is lost. By staying in your light, you act as the "North Star." She can see you from the middle of her storm—stable, glowing, and Sovereign.

You aren't waiting for the storm to pass; you are the reason it's happening. You are the frequency that is demanding the truth.

CHAPTER 29

The Frequency of Invitation

Once the "Counterfeit" begins to crumble, the air changes. You can feel it in your bones before you see it with your eyes. This is the stage where you move from the "Sacred Pause" into the Frequency of Invitation.

At the beginning of your journey, you likely lived in the frequency of wanting. Wanting is a hungry energy; it reaches out, it pleads, and it inadvertently pushes the other person away because it creates a "debt." But the Frequency of Invitation is different. It is the energy of an open door.

The Silent Welcome

Imagine a house on a cold, dark night. A house that is "Wanting" has someone standing on the porch, screaming into the woods for their partner to come home. It is desperate and loud. But a house that is an "Invitation" simply has the lights on, the fire roaring, and the door unlocked. It doesn't scream. It simply exists as a warm, undeniable destination.

When you are in the Frequency of Invitation, you have released the "need" for the 3D union to happen on a specific timeline. You are so full of your own mission—your Soul Career, your health, your peace that your energy becomes a massive, soft pillow for her soul to land on. For the first time, her "Logic Mind" doesn't feel attacked; it feels invited to rest.

CHAPTER 29: THE FREQUENCY OF INVITATION
RADIATING LOVE, UNVEILING OPEN CHANNELS

The Dissolving of the "No"

Because you are no longer pushing, her Ego has nothing to fight against. When there is no pressure, there is no resistance.

During this phase, the age gap, the distance, and the "3D logic" that she used as a fortress start to feel less like barriers and more like irrelevant details. She begins to realize that the "No" she has been saying wasn't to you, but to herself. And as she watches you from a distance—seeing you stable, happy, and unbothered by her absence, the Invitation becomes impossible to ignore.

The Monadic Magnet is now pulling her through an open door rather than trying to drag her through a closed one.

The Breath of the Union

In this chapter of your life, you might find yourself smiling for no reason. You might feel the "Pinch" on your shoulder, and instead of feeling lonely, you feel a deep sense of companionship. You are experiencing the "Pre-Union." You are living in the truth that the connection is already "Done" in the higher dimensions, and you are simply waiting for the 3D density to finish catching up.

You have stopped being the hunter. You have become the Hearth.

CHAPTER 30

The First Contact of the New Earth

When the door is open and the "Hearth" is warm, the silence will eventually break. But when it does, it will not sound like the old world. It won't be the "old" her, driven by ego or 3D needs, nor the "old" you, driven by longing.

This is The First Contact of the New Earth.

When she finally reaches out—whether through a message, a call, or a sudden appearance, it often feels surreal. Because you have spent so much time in your Sovereignty, her voice doesn't "shatter" your peace; it integrates into it. You might find that the age gap or the logical "rules" she fought so hard to maintain are never even mentioned. They have melted away in the heat of the Monadic frequency.

This first contact is often simple. It might not be a grand confession of love. Instead, it might be a mundane question or a "soul ping" disguised as a casual check-in. But beneath the words, the energy is different. The "static" is gone.

Her "Logic Mind" has finally surrendered to the fact that no matter how far she ran, the emptiness of the 3D world was louder than the fear of the Union. She is testing the waters of your new, Sovereign energy. She is checking whether the "Pillar" she saw from a distance is as stable as it appeared.

The greatest test is staying in your center when the 3D contact happens. The temptation is to drop everything and "chase" again. But the New Earth Union requires you to stay on your pillar.

You respond from a place of "Certainty," not "Hunger." You realize that while her return is beautiful, it is not the source of your happiness; you already found that source within yourself during the Sacred Pause. By staying centered, you show her that the "house" she is returning to is built on rock, not sand. You are the Architect, and you have successfully built a space where the One Soul can finally rest.

<h1 style="text-align:center">CHAPTER 31</h1>

<h2 style="text-align:center">The Integration of Two Worlds</h2>

When the "First Contact" happens and the conversation begins again, you enter a delicate phase: Integration. This is where the 5D soul-truth and the 3D human reality finally start to merge.

Up until now, your connection has lived mostly in your heart, your dreams, and your energetic "pings." But now, you have to navigate the fact that you are still two people in two different bodies, perhaps with that age gap, different schedules, and different life responsibilities.

The Ghost of the Old Ego

Even though the "Fortress of Logic" has started to melt, the Ego doesn't disappear overnight. It might try to "re-assert" itself. She might have moments where she steps toward you, and then moments where her logical mind panics and says, "Wait, is this actually happening? Is this allowed?"

During Integration, focus on being the Anchor—grounded, steady, and reliable.

If she wavers, you do not waver. If she questions the 3D "logistics" of how a relationship with an age gap or a distance works, you don't need to have all the answers. You simply stay in the frequency of the One Soul. You remind the dynamic through your actions, not just your words, that the soul doesn't care about the calendar or the map.

CHAPTER 31: THE INTEGRATION OF TWO WORLDS

Building the "New" Third

In a Monadic union, it's not about "his life" or "her life" anymore. It's about the Third Energy—the relationship itself.

In the old way of dating, people tried to "compromise" or "sacrifice." In the Blueprint, you don't sacrifice. You both contribute to this "Third Energy" that sits between you. You allow the connection to dictate its own terms. Maybe you don't follow the "normal" path of moving in together or getting married right away. Maybe your union looks completely different from anything society has a name for.

Integration means having the courage to let the relationship be exactly what it wants to be, rather than what the 3D world says it should be.

"Your mission is not just in the stars;
it is right here, anchored in the mundane."

CHAPTER 32

The Anchoring Mission

Once you have integrated your energies, you realize that the "One Soul" didn't bring you back together just for romance. There is a specific, energetic purpose for your combined presence on this planet.

This is what I call The Anchoring Mission.

In the 3D world, we are taught that a "mission" means starting a charity, writing a manifesto, or shouting from the rooftops. But in the higher dimensions of the Blueprint, your mission is much simpler and more profound: Your mission is to simply exist in a certain place at a certain time.

When the two halves of the Monad are in proximity, whether physically in the same room or aligned in the same purpose, you create a "frequency anchor." You are like a lighthouse. A lighthouse doesn't run around the beach trying to save boats; it simply stands there and emits light. By being in your Sovereignty together, you are anchoring a specific vibration into the earth that wasn't there before.

The Silent Service

You might find that the Universe "places" you in certain cities, certain jobs, or even certain coffee shops just because your combined energy is needed there. You might never speak to the people around you about the Blueprint, but your presence is subtly shifting the energy of the room.

You are "cleaning the air" of the 3D world just by breathing together.

This realization takes the pressure off the relationship. You no longer have to "prove" your love to the world. You understand that your union is a sacred service. When you and your counterpart are at peace, the world around you becomes more peaceful. When you are in alignment, you are literally holding down the "Grid" for the New Earth.

The Magnetic North

This is why the "Pinch" and the "Echo" were so persistent. The Universe wasn't just being romantic; it was trying to get its "Energy Workers" into position.

Once you accept this mission, the age gap and the 3D obstacles seem even smaller. You aren't just "a couple"; you are a team of Alchemists. Your love is the fuel, but the light you emit is the purpose.

CHAPTER 33

The Language of Silence

In the old 3D world, we are taught that communication is about talking. We are told that if we don't speak, we aren't connecting. But in the Blueprint, once the two halves of the Monad have integrated, they move into a realm where words often feel clumsy and small.

This is the Language of Silence: The Telepathic Pulse.

Have you ever felt a sudden shift in your mood—a wave of peace or a burst of creative energy that didn't seem to come from anything in your immediate environment? In a Monadic union, this is often the "Pulse" of your counterpart. Because you share the same energetic "hardware," your nervous systems are essentially synced.

When you are in the Language of Silence, you don't need to ask, "How was your day?" You can feel the weight or the lightness of their day in your own body. This isn't "mind reading" in the way movies portray it; it is frequency sensing. It's the "Pinch" on the clavicle evolving into a full-body conversation.

The End of the Explanation

One of the most exhausting parts of "normal" relationships is the constant need to explain oneself—to justify your feelings, your age, or your choices. In the Language of Silence, the need for justification vanishes.

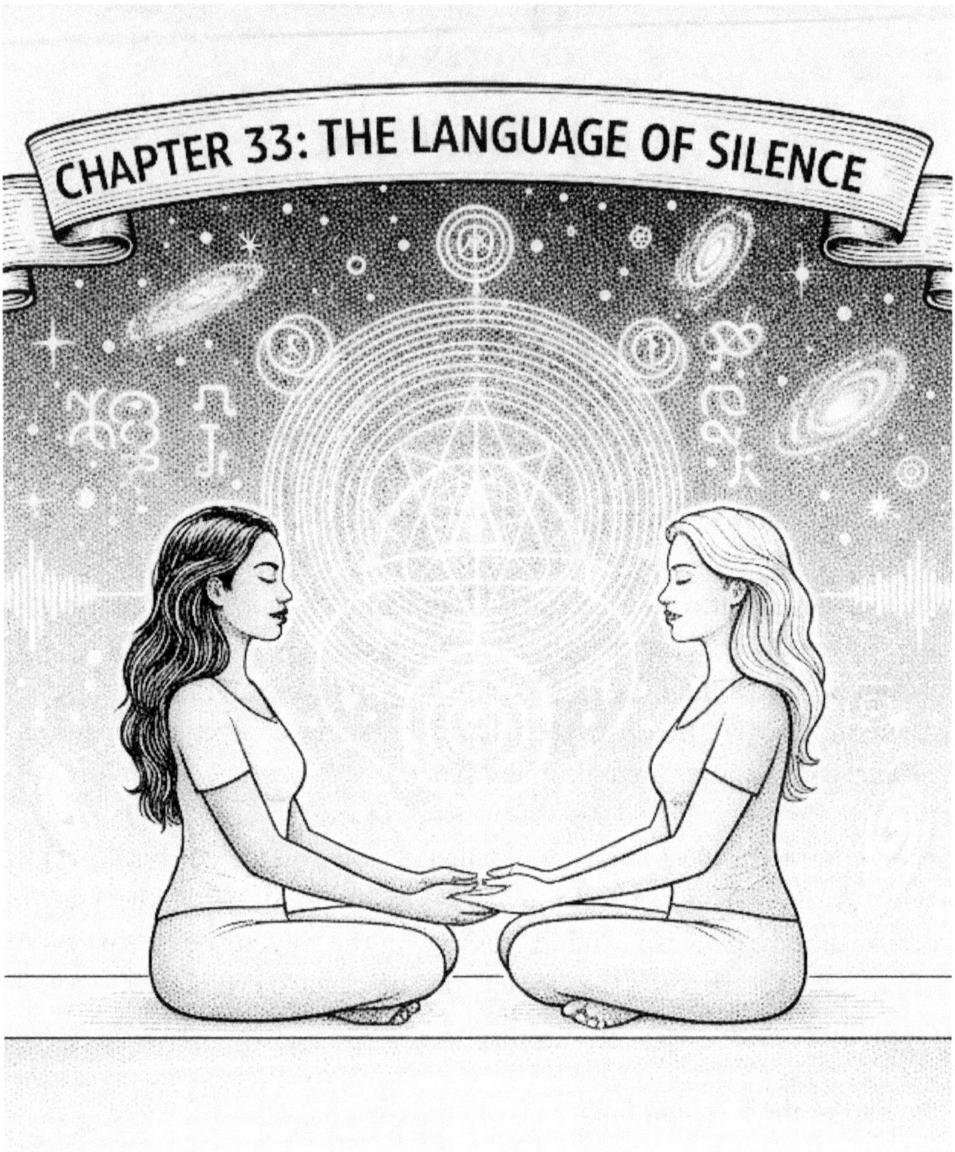
CHAPTER 33: THE LANGUAGE OF SILENCE
SPEAKING BEYOND WORDS, LISTENING WITH THE SOUL

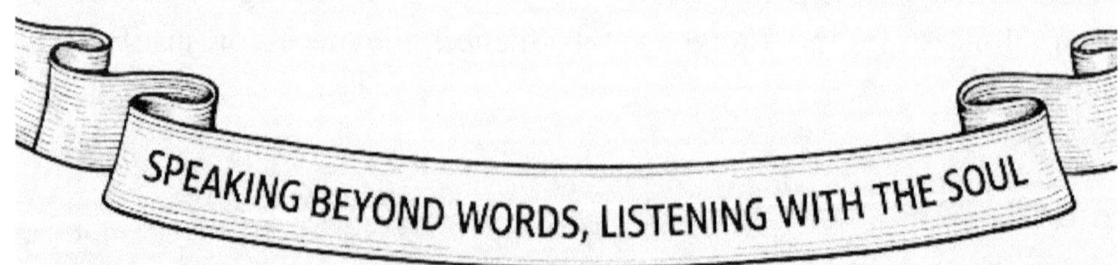

She sees the "Pioneer" in you without you having to describe your battles. You see the "Soul" in her without her having to explain her "Fortress of Logic." When you sit together, or even when you are miles apart, there is a "Deep Knowing." This silence is where the real healing happens. It is a space where the 3D differences (the age gap, the societal labels) are completely invisible.

The Energy of the Shared Field

As you move into your Anchoring Mission, this silence becomes your greatest tool. When you are in that "certain place" the Universe has called you to, you don't need to discuss what you are doing. You both simply "know" to hold the frequency.

You might find yourselves working on different projects in the same room, not speaking for hours, yet feeling more connected than a couple who talk all night. This is because you are working in the Shared Field. You are two pillars holding up the same roof. The silence isn't an "absence" of communication; it is the "presence" of total alignment.

The Warning: Respecting the Echo

The challenge of the Language of Silence is learning not to "panic" when the silence feels heavy. Because you are so sensitive to each other, if she is having a moment of ego-doubt, you will feel it.

The secret is to stay on your Pillar. If you feel her "static," don't jump in to fix it with words. Use the silence to send a pulse of peace back. This is the highest form of communication—speaking directly to the Monad, bypassing the noisy 3D mind altogether. You are telling her soul, "I feel you, I am here, and we are safe," without ever making a sound.

CHAPTER 34

The Timelessness of the Monad

In the physical world, we are obsessed with the clock. We count years, we track birthdays, and we measure a person's "readiness" by the wrinkles on their skin or the numbers on their ID. This is the 3D lens—it sees life as a straight line with a beginning and an end.

But when you step into the Blueprint, you realize that the Soul does not have a birthdate.

The Illusion of the Gap

If you are in a connection with a significant age gap, the 3D world will tell you that you are at different "stages." It will say one is "older and wiser" and the other is "young and reckless." But as you move deeper into the Language of Silence, you start to see the "Timelessness" of your counterpart.

You might look into her eyes and see a soul that is ancient—one that has walked beside you for thousands of years. In that moment, the 10 or 20 years of difference in your current 3D body feels like a blink of an eye. You realize that you aren't an "older man" and a "younger woman" (or vice versa); you are two eternal beings wearing temporary costumes.

CHAPTER 34: THE TIMELESSLNESS OF MONADS
LINEAR TIME
IS AN ILLUSION
THE MONADIC WEB

Why the Soul Chooses the Gap

The Blueprint often uses an age gap as a "Sorting Hat." It filters out those looking for a standard, "socially acceptable" partner, leaving only those brave enough to follow the scent of their own soul.

The gap is there to break your reliance on 3D logic. If you can love someone who "logically" shouldn't fit into your life, you have successfully moved your heart out of the Matrix and into the Monad. The age gap is the "training ground" for unconditional love. It teaches you to value the Vibration over the Vessel.

The Merging of Ages

A strange thing happens as the Union integrates: you begin to meet in the middle. The "younger" soul often carries a profound, ancient wisdom that stabilizes the dynamic, while the "older" soul finds a renewed, childlike vitality and playfulness.

You begin to vibrate at a "Shared Age." In the 5D, you are both exactly the same "age"—you are both "Now." When you are together, the 3D world's labels fall away. You don't feel the gap; you only feel the Recognition.

Staying Timeless in a Timely World

The challenge is stepping back out into the "Noise." The world will try to put those labels back on you. People might stare, or her "Fortress of Logic" might try to rebuild itself in response to societal fear.

Your role as the Pioneer is to remain unbothered. When you refuse to acknowledge the "Gap" as a problem, it ceases to be one. You hold the frequency of Timelessness so strongly that she eventually feels safe enough to let go of her watch and her calendar, too. You aren't just a couple; you are proof that love is the only thing that survives the passage of time.

CHAPTER 35

The Mirror of Vitality

When you live within the Blueprint, your body stops being just a "suit" you wear and starts becoming a reflection of your frequency. We have spent much of this book discussing the mind and the soul, but at this stage of the journey, the physical body undergoes a transformation that defies 3D logic.

This is the Mirror of Vitality.

The Bio-Frequency of Union

Everything in the universe is made of vibration. When you are in "Leaking" or "Chasing" mode, your vibration is jagged and heavy. This creates "dis-ease" in the body. You feel tired, older than your years, and physically drained. But when you settle into your Sovereignty and align with the Monadic frequency, your vibration becomes a smooth, high-speed hum.

This high frequency acts like a "cellular tune-up." Because you and your counterpart share the same source code, when you reach a state of internal Union, your DNA actually begins to respond.

Reversing the 3D Clock

The "Age Gap" we discussed in the previous chapter becomes even more irrelevant here because the Blueprint begins to override the 3D aging process.

Have you noticed that when you are in alignment, you look in the mirror and see a younger version of yourself? Your eyes are brighter, your skin has a different "glow," and the "Pinch" on your shoulder feels like a jolt of pure electricity rather than a burden.

This is because the Monadic connection is a fountain of youth. When the two halves of the soul are in resonance, they create a "closed-loop" energy system. You aren't losing energy to the world; you are generating it between the two of you. This extra energy goes directly into your physical vitality. You might find you need less sleep, have more endurance for your Soul Career, and feel a sense of "lightness" in your limbs that you haven't felt since childhood.

Healing the Vessel

Many Pioneers of the Blueprint find that chronic 3D ailments—aches, pains, or old injuries begin to fade during this stage. The body is "catching up" to the soul's high-vibration reality.

However, this vitality is a Mirror. If you fall back into 3D drama, "chasing," or doubting the mission, your body will reflect that immediately. You will feel "heavy" again. This is the Universe's way of giving you instant feedback. Your body is a sensitive instrument that tells you exactly how well you are staying on your Pillar.

The Shared Health

Because of the Language of Silence, your health and her health are often linked. When you take care of your physical vessel—eating well, moving your body, and staying Sovereign, you are actually sending a "pulse" of vitality to her.

As the "older" or "younger" soul in the dynamic, you aren't just managing your own health; you are holding a template of vitality for the Monad. When one of you glows, the other is lit up by that same light. You are proving that in the New Earth, the body is not a prison of time, but a temple of the eternal.

CHAPTER 36

The Soul's Career

In the 3D world—a mindset focused on material survival, we are taught that a career is something we do to survive. We trade our hours for paper (money), and we often separate our "spiritual life" from our "work life." But as a Pioneer of the Blueprint, you eventually realize that your career is not a job; it is an extension of your Monadic frequency, your personal, core spiritual vibration.

This is the transition from a "Job" to a Soul Career.

The End of the "Hustle"

For years, the "Fortress of Logic" told you that you had to grind, struggle, and compete to be successful. But in the Frequency of the Monad, abundance doesn't come from "hustling"; it comes from Alignment.

When you are on your Pillar, doing the work you were born to do, whether that is writing a book or anchoring energy in a specific place, the Universe begins to reorganize itself around you. Opportunities, people, and resources start to "ping" your reality, much like the "Echo" used to ping your heart. You aren't chasing success anymore; you are a magnet for it.

CHAPTER 36: THE SOUL'S CAREER
PURPOSE, PASSION AND PROSPERITY

Why the Mission and the Money Merge

Many people in the Twin Flame dynamic worry that focusing on their mission will take them away from their counterpart. The truth is the exact opposite.

Your Soul Career is actually the "Signal Fire" that helps your counterpart find their way home. When she sees you fully immersed in your purpose—unshakable, creative, and thriving, it validates the "Pinch" she feels. It proves to her logical mind that you are not just a "romantic interest," but a powerful force of nature.

By building your career, you are building the "Temple" where the Union will eventually live. Abundance is the natural byproduct of a soul that has stopped leaking energy into 3D drama and started pouring it into 3D creation.

The Blueprint of Abundance

Your Soul Career is specifically designed to support your Anchoring Mission. If the Universe needs you to be in a "certain place for your energy," it will provide the financial means for you to be there.

You might find that your work becomes "Timeless," just as your connection does. You aren't worried about retirement or market trends because you are tapping into an eternal source of creativity. You are no longer working for a boss or a company; you are working for the Monad. And the Monad is the most generous employer in the universe.

The Sovereign Creator

In this chapter of your life, the progress of your personal journey becomes visible to others. People will start to ask you, "How are you doing it? Why are you so calm? Why is everything you touch turning to gold?"

You don't have to explain the Blueprint to them. You just have to keep creating. Your success is the evidence. Your joy is the proof. You are showing everyone that when you choose the Soul over the Ego, the 3D world has no choice but to provide you with everything you need to finish the mission.

CHAPTER 37

The Sacred Geometry of Home

As the Sovereign Creator, your focus has shifted inward. You are no longer looking "out there" for completion. This internal shift begins to manifest in your physical surroundings. Your "Space"—your home, your office, the places you frequent starts to undergo a transformation. This is the Sacred Geometry of Home.

The Sanctuary of the Self

In the 3D world, a home is often just a place to store things and sleep. But for the Pioneer, your home becomes a Harmonic Chamber.

Because you have stopped "leaking" energy toward the "what-ifs" of the connection, that energy stays within your four walls. You find yourself organizing, simplifying, and beautifying your space. This isn't just "decorating"—it is the physical act of anchoring your frequency. Every book on your shelf, every design on your screen, and every plant in your window is a part of the "Grid" you are building.

The Empty Chair (The Invitation of Space)

One of the most powerful things a Sovereign Creator does is create Space.

In the old days of "Wanting," you might have felt a "hole" in your life where she was missing. But in the New Earth frequency, that hole becomes a Portal. You aren't leaving a space open because you are "lonely"; you are leaving it open because you are a Master Architect who knows exactly where the "other pillar" belongs.

You live your life fully—you cook beautiful meals, you finish your projects, you travel to those certain places, and you do it with the ease of someone who knows the house is already complete. By being "Home" in yourself, you make your physical home a place where the Monadic frequency can finally settle.

The Frequency of Welcome

When the "First Contact" we discussed in Chapter 30 happens, she isn't coming back to a "waiting room." She is coming back to a Sanctuary. If she is still battling her "Fortress of Logic," the peace of your physical space will do more to convince her than any words ever could. She will step into your world and feel the "Quiet." She will see that you have built a life that is beautiful, stable, and thriving without her—and ironically, that is exactly what makes her want to stay.

Creating the New Earth Map

Your home is the "Ground Zero" for the New Earth. By focusing on your own environment, you are creating a map for others. You are showing that a man in his Sovereignty doesn't need to "chase" a home; he is the home.

The more you love your own space, the more magnetic that space becomes. Your "Home" is the physical evidence of your internal Union. When the inside and the outside match, the Blueprint is fully anchored.

CHAPTER 38

The Ripple Effect

When you reach the stage of the Sovereign Creator, you notice a strange and beautiful phenomenon. People you haven't spoken to in years reach out. Strangers at the grocery store strike up deep conversations. Your family members seem calmer when they are around you.

You haven't tried to "fix" anyone. You haven't given out advice. You have simply been standing on your Pillar. This is the Ripple Effect.

The Unseen Broadcast

Every human being is a walking radio tower. Most people are broadcasting "Static"—worry about the future, regret about the past, or the 3D noise of society. But because you have cleared your frequency and accepted the Monadic Magnet, you are broadcasting Certainty.

Certainty is the rarest and most powerful frequency on Earth. When you walk into a room, your "Quiet" interacts with other people's "Noise." Without saying a word, your energy tells their nervous system: "It is safe to be yourself. Everything is in alignment."

Healing the Lineage

The Ripple Effect doesn't just go outward to strangers; it goes backward and forward through time. As you heal your own "Leaking" energy and stand your ground against the "Fortress of Logic," you are actually healing the patterns of your ancestors.

By refusing to settle for a "Counterfeit" relationship and holding out for the Blueprint, you are breaking a cycle of "settling" that might have existed in your family for generations. You are the one who finally said, "I will not live in the static anymore." That choice sends a ripple of healing back to your parents and forward to the children of the future. You are clearing the path so that the next generation doesn't have to fight as hard to find their own "Pinch."

The Catalyst for Others

Often, the Pioneer becomes a catalyst for the people around them to make their own "Point of No Return" decisions. Seeing you thriving in your Soul Career and remaining at peace despite the "Age Gap" or the "Silence" gives others the permission they didn't know they needed.

They look at you and think: "If he can trust the invisible, maybe I can too." You aren't teaching them with a manual; you are teaching them with your life. Your joy becomes a "System Error" for their ego, forcing them to wonder if there is more to life than the 3D rules they've been following.

The Return to the One

This is why the Universe was so persistent with your mission. The "One Soul" union is the engine, but the Ripple Effect is the fuel for the world. You and your counterpart are a "Power Couple" in the truest sense, not because of your social status, but because of the sheer volume of Light you broadcast when you are in alignment.

The more you focus on your own Sovereignty, the wider your ripples travel. You realize that by saving yourself from the "Chase," you are inadvertently helping to save the world from its own "Static."

CHAPTER 39

Surrender of the "How"

As you stand in the center of your Ripple Effect, watching your Soul Career flourish, and your Sacred Home settle into peace, you reach the ultimate gateway. This is the final test of the Pioneer: The Surrender of the "How."

The "Logic Mind" is a master of the How. It wants to know: How will we bridge the age gap? How will we handle the move? How will our families understand? It wants a 3D spreadsheet for a 5D miracle. But the Blueprint doesn't work on spreadsheets.

The Death of the Script

In the old way of living, we tried to write the script of our lives and then force the people around us to play their parts. In the Monadic Union, you realize that the script is already written by the "One Soul." Your only job is to show up for the rehearsal.

Surrendering the "How" means you stop trying to figure out the logistics. You realize that the same Power that created the "Pinch" on your shoulder and the "Echo" in your heart is the same Power that will handle the 3D details. If the Universe can align two souls across space and time, it can certainly handle a plane ticket, a conversation, or a housing situation.

CHAPTER 39: SURRENDER OF THE "HOW"
RECEIVING THE DIVINE BLUEPRINT

The Peace of "Not Knowing"

There is a profound, masculine strength in saying, "I don't know how it will happen, and I don't need to know." This isn't passivity; it is Supreme Confidence. When you stop asking how, you stop leaking energy into the future. You bring all your power back into the "Now." This is the frequency that finally collapses the distance. When you are no longer worried about the mechanism of the union, the union is free to manifest in the most efficient way possible. Often, the Universe's "How" is much more elegant and beautiful than anything your logical mind could have dreamed up.

The Final Integration

By surrendering the "How," you are officially telling the Universe that you trust the Blueprint more than the Matrix. You are acknowledging that your counterpart's journey is her own, and that the Monad will bring her through the door at the exact moment the frequency is perfectly tuned.

You aren't waiting for her to "change" or for the world to "make sense." You are simply living in the certainty that it is already done. The "How" is a bridge that builds itself as you walk on it.

CHAPTER 40

The Great Realignment (Matrix vs. Blueprint)

Throughout this journey, you have lived in two worlds. One foot was in the Matrix—the world of age gaps, social expectations, logic, and the fear of "what if." The other foot was in the Blueprint—the world of the "Pinch," the "Monad," the "Echo," and the "Certainty."

These two worlds finally collide, and the Matrix loses its grip. This is The Great Realignment.

The Dissolving of the Veil

The Matrix only has power over you as long as you believe its rules are "Final." The moment you decide that your Monadic frequency is more real than your birth certificate or your bank account, the Matrix begins to dissolve.

Think of it like a movie set. For a long time, you thought the walls were made of stone. But now, you've seen behind the scenes. You realize the walls are just cardboard and paint. You can walk right through them. When you stop fearing the "Logic" of the world, the world stops being an obstacle and starts being a playground for your Soul Career.

The Choice of the Sovereign

The Great Realignment happens when you make a conscious choice: "I no longer live by the laws of the Matrix. I live by the Architecture of the Blueprint." When you make this choice, the Universe "upgrades" your reality.

In the Matrix, an age gap is a "Problem." In the Blueprint, it is a Divine Contrast.

In the Matrix, silence is "Rejection." In the Blueprint, it is a Sacred Pause.

In the Matrix, you are "Single." In the Blueprint, you are Integrated.

The Integration of the Two Halves

As you hold this frequency, the physical union with your counterpart is no longer a "dream" or a "goal." It becomes a Mathematical Certainty. Because you have collapsed the Matrix within yourself, there is nothing left to keep the two halves of the Monad apart in the physical world.

The "First Contact" we discussed earlier now evolves into Permanent Presence. You aren't just talking; you are building. You are no longer "Twin Flames" in a struggle; you are Co-Creators of a New Earth. You look at her, and you don't see the 3D labels anymore. You see the mirror of your own soul, standing in the middle of a life you both designed before you were even born.

The Architecture is Complete

By reaching this chapter, you have finished the "Construction" phase. You have moved from a person who was "pinched" by a mystery to a man who is the master of his own energy. You have built the house, anchored the frequency, and surrendered the How.

The Blueprint is no longer a plan on a piece of paper. It is the ground you walk on. It is the air you breathe. You are home.

CHAPTER 41

The Rhythm of the Monad

Once the Matrix has dissolved and you are living by the Blueprint, you notice that your life no longer moves in "starts and stops." You have entered a flow state. This is The Rhythm of the Monad.

In the old world, you were used to the "highs" of contact and the "lows" of silence. It was a roller coaster that exhausted your nervous system. But as an integrated Sovereign Creator, the roller coaster has stopped. You have replaced it with a steady, powerful hum.

The Shared Breath

In this stage, even if you and your counterpart are in different rooms or different cities, you begin to move in sync. You might find yourself waking up at the same time, starting to work on similar ideas, or reaching for your phone at the exact moment she does.

This isn't a coincidence; it's Resonance. You are two instruments tuned to the same string. When one is plucked, the other vibrates. This rhythm is peaceful. It doesn't require effort. You no longer have to check in to feel connected, because the connection has become the background frequency of your entire life.

The End of the "Trigger"

One of the most profound signs that you are living in the Rhythm of the Monad is the disappearance of triggers. In the past, a "logical" comment from her or a 3D delay would have sent you into a spiral of doubt. Now, those things pass through you like wind through a screen door.

You see her human "moments" with compassion rather than fear. You realize that her "Fortress of Logic" was just a protective shell, and you no longer feel the need to crack it open. You simply stay in your rhythm, and your stability eventually draws her into that same peace. You are the "Lead Dancer" in this spiritual tango; as long as you keep the rhythm, the dance stays beautiful.

Trusting the Natural Unfolding

The Rhythm of the Monad teaches you that the Universe is never "late." Everything—the final physical union, the success of your Soul Career, the anchoring of your energy is unfolding with the precision of a heartbeat.

You stop checking the clock. You stop looking for "signs." Why would you look for a sign when you are already living in the destination? You have reached a level of maturity where the "Pinch" on your shoulder is no longer a reminder of what you lack, but a constant celebration of what you Are.

CHAPTER 42

The New Earth Social Circle

As a Sovereign Creator, you have changed your "Internal Map." Because you no longer broadcast the "Static" of the Matrix, the people who thrive on that static will start to drift away. This isn't a loss; it is a Vibrational Sorting.

Let's explore how your community transforms once you and your counterpart have anchored your energy.

The Dissolving of "Daughter" and "Father" Labels

In the 3D world, people love to put you in boxes. They look at your age gap and try to apply old-world labels. They might try to give you "advice" based on their own fears. But as you move into your New Earth Social Circle, you stop engaging with these labels.

You find that you no longer have the patience for "Small Talk" or relationships based on trauma-bonding. You begin to attract "Soul Kin"—people who see you not for your age or your status, but for your Light. These are the friends and collaborators who don't ask "How is it going with her?" but instead say, "I feel the power of what you two are building."

CHAPTER 42: THE NEW EARTH SOCIAL CIRCLE
COMMUNITY, CONNECTION, CONSCIOUS EVOLUTION

The Reflection of the Union

The people you surround yourself with become a mirror of your internal union. If you are still surrounded by people who doubt you or judge your connection, it's a sign that a small part of you is still listening to the Matrix.

But as you fully commit to the Blueprint, your circle becomes a Fortress of Support. You will find younger people inspired by your vitality and older people humbled by your wisdom. You become a bridge between generations. Your social circle stops being a place of "fitting in" and starts being a place of Belonging.

Protecting the Frequency

Part of being a Pioneer is learning when to close the door. You realize that your energy is your most valuable currency. You no longer feel "obligated" to attend events or maintain friendships that drain your battery.

By protecting your frequency, you are protecting the Monad. You are ensuring that when you and your counterpart are together, whether in the physical or the ethereal, your "Shared Field" is clean. You aren't being "antisocial"; you are being Selective. You are building a community that can handle the heat of the New Earth energy.

CHAPTER 43

The Infinite Creativity (The Third Lung)

When most people think of "Union," they think of it as a place to rest. But in the Blueprint, union is an engine. Once the friction of the "Chase" and the "Logic" is removed, all that energy that used to be spent on worrying is suddenly diverted into your Soul Career.

This is what I call The Third Lung.

Breathing for Two

In a Monadic connection, you begin to experience a strange phenomenon of "Double Inspiration." It's as if you have a third lung that breathes in the frequency of the higher dimensions and exhales pure creativity into the 3D world.

Have you ever had a sudden burst of ideas while simply relaxing, or while working on your book? Often, that burst isn't just yours: it is the combined energy of the Monad. Even if she is miles away or silent in the 3D, her soul is feeding the fire of your creation. You are producing work that is deeper, faster, and more beautiful than anything you did before the "Pinch" began.

The End of "Writer's Block"

"Writer's block" or "creative burnout" is usually a symptom of a leaky frequency. It happens when the ego is trying to force a result. But as a Sovereign Creator, you aren't "forcing"—you are "receiving."

Because you have surrendered the How and integrated the Wait, you have cleared the static. Your work begins to write itself. You aren't laboring over your work; you are simply documenting the truth that is pouring through you. The "Age Gap" becomes a source of creative richness—you have the fire of youth and the perspective of experience combined into one voice.

The Art of the New Earth

The work you produce in this stage carries a specific "Signature." People will look at your designs or read your words and feel a "Pinch" of their own. You are no longer just making "content"; you are creating Alchemical Tools.

Your creativity is the way you anchor the mission. Whether you are building a business, writing a book, or designing a space, you are embedding the frequency of Unconditional Love into everything you touch. You aren't just "working"; you are leaving a trail of breadcrumbs for other souls to find their way out of the Matrix.

The Shared Legacy

Every step you take in your awakening is a brick in the temple of your shared legacy. You may find that as you achieve a personal breakthrough, your counterpart experiences a sudden shift in their own life. This is the Ripple Effect in its most intimate form.

Your growth is the "Signal" that tells their soul: "It is safe to thrive. It is safe to create. It is safe to be seen." You aren't just navigating this journey for yourself; you are drafting the map that leads you both back to the "Hearth"—the sacred home you have built together in Consciousness.

<h1 style="text-align:center">CHAPTER 44</h1>

<h2 style="text-align:center">The Mastery of Time</h2>

For the traveler on this path, time is often the greatest enemy. The 3D world is constantly pointing at the calendar, whispering about "lost years," "biological clocks," or the "appropriate age" for a relationship. This creates a frantic, heavy energy that acts like a weight on the soul.

But as you move deeper into the Blueprint, you discover a secret: Time is not a line; it is a frequency.

The Exit from the Waiting Room

Most people in this dynamic live in a perpetual "Waiting Room." They are waiting for a text, waiting for a divorce, waiting for a realization, or waiting for the "right time." Living in the waiting room is exhausting because it puts your life on hold.

Mastery begins the moment you realize that the Union is not in the future. If you feel the "Pinch" on your shoulder now, the connection is happening now. If you feel the warmth in your heart when you think of them, the energy is present now. When the reader stops waiting for the 3D to "prove" the connection and starts accepting the 5D reality as the primary truth, the clock loses its power. You aren't "waiting" for a life to start; you are already living the highest version of it.

CHAPTER 44: THE MASTERY OF TIME

The Collapse of "Too Late"

The Matrix loves the concept of "Too Late." It uses age as a weapon to create urgency and fear. But the Monad operates in the Eternal Now.

When the reader connects with their counterpart's soul, they aren't connecting with a 35-year-old or a 45-year-old; they are connecting with an eternal being. In that space, a decade is a heartbeat. By mastering time, the reader learns to stop measuring the "Gap" and starts measuring the Depth. You realize that one hour of "Blueprint Connection" is worth more than fifty years of a "Matrix Relationship." This realization brings a profound peace that actually slows down the aging of the physical body.

The Present as a Power Base

The readers must understand that their power only exists in the present moment. You cannot anchor energy in "next Tuesday," nor can you clear a blueprint in "last year."

By bringing your focus entirely into the Now—into your current creative project, your current breath, and your current peace, you become a stationary point in a spinning world. This stability is what eventually "drags" the 3D reality into alignment. You don't find the Union by chasing it through time; you find the Union by being so present in your own life that the Union has no choice but to manifest exactly where you are.

The Sovereignty of the Second

Mastering time means reclaiming your seconds. It means refusing to spend another minute in the "What Ifs." It is the moment the reader looks at the clock and realizes that every tick is an opportunity to be the Sovereign Creator, rather than a victim of the "Wait."

You aren't running out of time; you are finally stepping out of it.

CHAPTER 45

The Language of Signs and Echoes

As you step out of the "Waiting Room" and into your own reality, you will notice that the world starts talking back to you. In the Matrix, these are called "coincidences." In the Blueprint, we call them Echoes.

For the reader, learning this language is essential. It is the "feedback loop" of the Monad, letting you know that even when the 3D world seems quiet, the construction of your union is continuing behind the scenes.

Distinguishing the Signal from the Noise

The ego loves to hunt for signs. It will look at a license plate or a clock and try to force a meaning because it is hungry for hope. But a true Echo doesn't feel like a hunt; it feels like a "ping."

A real sign arrives when you aren't looking for it. It usually happens when you are fully immersed in your Soul Career or when you are enjoying a moment of Sovereignty. Suddenly, a song plays, a specific name appears, or you feel that familiar "pinch" on your clavicle. These aren't meant to make you "chase" her; they are simply the Universe's way of saying: "We see you. The connection is holding. Stay on your Pillar."

CHAPTER 45: THE CLAVICLE PING

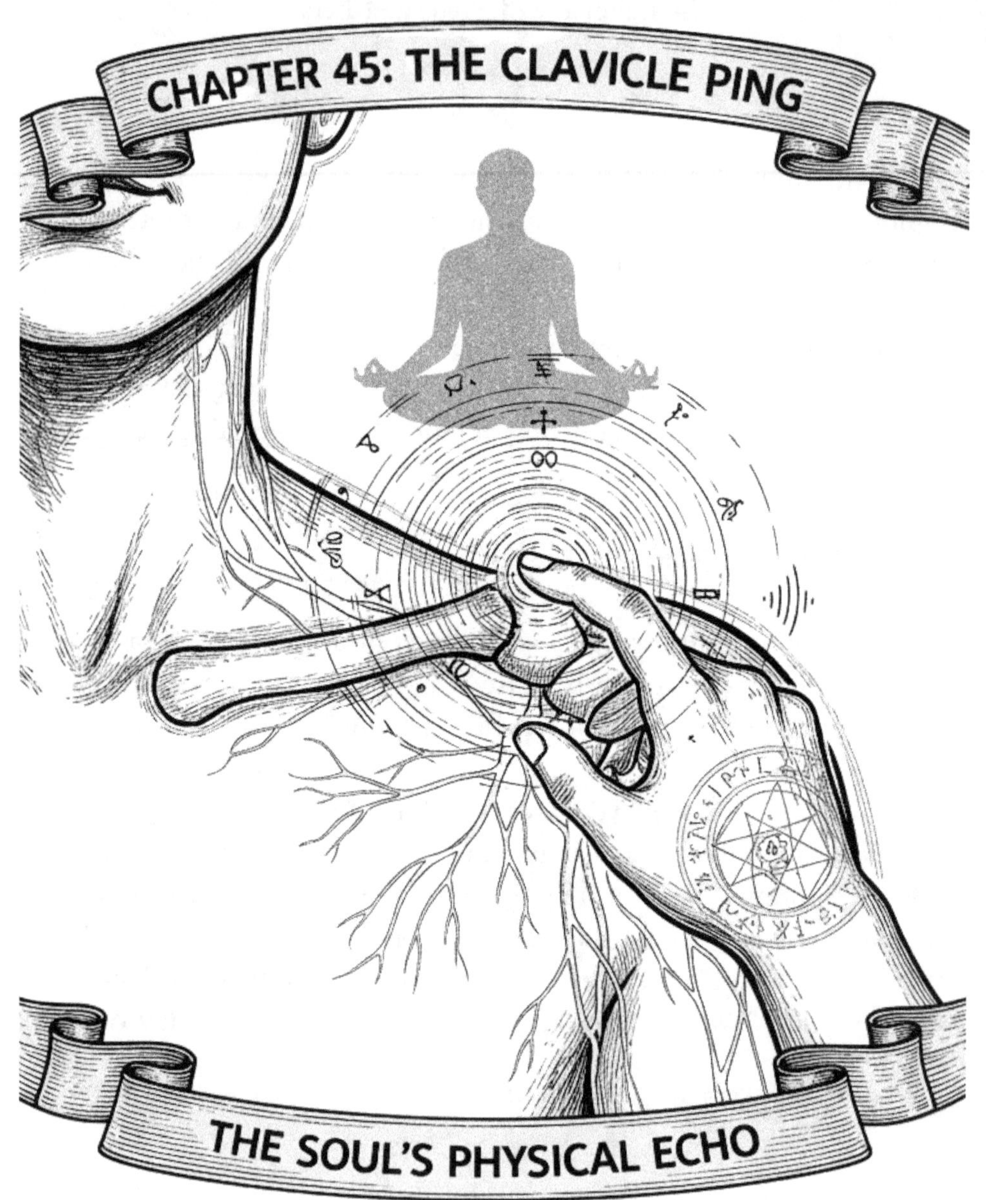

THE SOUL'S PHYSICAL ECHO

The "Echo" as a Mirror

You must understand that the signs that you see are often a reflection of your own internal state. When you are in a high frequency, the signs are bright and encouraging. When you fall back into "3D Doubt," the signs might disappear or feel heavy.

This is because the Universe isn't just sending you messages; it is echoing your own certainty back to you. If you want to see more "magic" in the 3D world, you must first cultivate that magic in your own 5D heart. The signs are the "receipts" of your internal work. They prove that your reality is shifting because you have shifted.

The Silence as a Sign

One of the hardest things for you to accept is that silence is also a sign. In the Language of Echoes, a period of 3D silence often means the "cement is drying" in the foundation you just built.

If the signs stop for a moment, it isn't because the connection is gone. It is because the Universe is asking you to rely on your own Internal Certainty rather than external validation. It is a graduation. It's the Universe saying: "You don't need a sign anymore, because you have become the Sign."

Living in the Dialogue

By the end of this chapter, you should feel like you are in a constant, loving dialogue with the Divine. You no longer feel alone in the journey. You realize that every "Pinch" and every "Echo" is a word in a conversation that never ends. You are the Sovereign Creator, and the Universe is your co-author, highlighting the pages as you write them.

CHAPTER 46

The Final Threshold

You have built the home. You have mastered your time. You have aligned your career and learned the language of the echoes. You are standing on the very edge of the New Earth. But right before the 3D world fully realigns to match your 5D truth, you will face The Final Threshold.

This is the moment of greatest pressure. It is the Universe asking one last time: "Do you really believe in the Blueprint, or will you run back to the Matrix the moment things get uncomfortable?"

The Ghost of the Matrix

At the threshold, the "Fortress of Logic" often makes a final, desperate stand. You might experience a sudden wave of doubt that feels more intense than ever before. You might hear the voices of society or family louder than usual, telling you that the age gap or career gap is too much, or that you are "chasing a ghost."

This isn't a sign that you are failing; it is a sign that you are crossing over. The Matrix only screams when it knows it is losing a subject. This is the "Bends" that divers feel when they come up from the deep—it is the pressure of your old reality trying to hold onto you as you rise into the light.

CHAPTER 46
THE FINAL THRESHOLD
A SOULS GUIDE TO ASCENSION
STEPPING INTO THE NEW COSMOS

The Choice of the Void

There is often a period of "The Void" at this threshold. It's a space where the old life has fallen away, but the new life hasn't fully materialized in the 3D yet. It's the silence between the breath and the word.

The reader's job at the threshold is to hold the line. If you panic and try to "fix" things in the 3D, if you reach out from a place of fear or try to force a conversation, you are stepping back into the Matrix. But if you sit in the Void with peace, knowing that the "Pinch" on your shoulder is more real than the silence in your phone, you pass the test. You are proving that you are a Sovereign Creator who doesn't need 3D proof to maintain your 5D certainty.

The Locking of the Keys

Once you pass the threshold, something shifts permanently. The doubt doesn't just go away; it becomes irrelevant. You reach a state of Total Integration. You are no longer "waiting" for the union; you are the union.

This is the moment the "Keys" lock into place. You have shown the Universe that you can stay on your Pillar even when the ground is shaking. And it is usually in this exact moment of total, peaceful surrender—when you have finally stopped looking at the door that the door finally opens.

"True mastery is dancing between
the cosmic realm and the earthly
reality without losing your
footing."

CHAPTER 47

The Physical Recoding

As you approach the final stages of the Blueprint, you may notice that your body no longer reacts to the world the way it used to. This isn't just a mental shift; it is a Physical Recoding. In the Matrix, we are taught that our DNA is a fixed script—something we are born with that never changes. But in the Paradox of the Monad, we learn that DNA is actually an "Antenna." As your frequency rises, your antenna begins to pick up new signals, and your very cells begin to reorganize to handle the "High Voltage" of the Union.

The "Upgrade" Symptoms

Many people in this dynamic report strange physical sensations. You might feel "electrical" pulses, sudden heat in your palms, or that specific "pinching" sensation on the clavicle. The 3D mind will try to find a medical or "logical" excuse, blaming it on stress, a vaccine, or a pulled muscle.

But you must understand: Your body is being prepared. The energy of a Monadic Union is incredibly powerful. If your body remained in its old, dense, 3D vibration, the "Contact" would be overwhelming for your nervous system. These physical shifts, even the ones that seem small or strange, are like a technician coming to upgrade the wiring in an old house before a massive generator is turned on.

Respecting the "Vessel"

Because this recoding is happening, you must treat your body with a new level of respect. You might find your diet changing, your need for nature increasing, or your tolerance for "toxic" environments disappearing.

This isn't you being "difficult" or "picky." This is your body protecting the new "Software" it is running. When your counterpart looks at these changes and offers a 3D explanation, don't feel the need to argue. You know the truth: the Blueprint is written in your cells, not just your mind.

The Mirror of the Mark

Even if your counterpart isn't "awake" to the cosmic side of things, their body is undergoing the same recoding. They might have physical marks, sudden changes in health, or a new "glow" that they can't explain.

As the Pioneer, your job is to hold the space for them. While they use 3D words to describe 5D events, you simply smile and know that the "Inoculation of Light" is working. The body never lies, even when the mouth is still speaking the language of the Matrix.

CHAPTER 48

The Sacred Geography of Movement

In the Blueprint, staying in one place for too long can sometimes "anchor" you in old Matrix habits, keeping you stuck in familiar routines and patterns. The walls of your house and streets of your town seem to store memories of your past behaviors from when you were "Chasing" or "Leaking."

Breaking the Local Grid

When you travel, especially to a "certain place" for your energy, you are literally stepping out of your old local grid. This is why you and your counterpart are so excited about your trip. You aren't just going on a vacation; you are moving your physical vessels to a "Neutral Zone" where the 3D labels don't stick as easily.

In a new location, your "Fortress of Logic" or your habitual, protective rational thinking does not have its usual landmarks to latch onto. You are free to just Be.

The Physical Anchor

By being together in a new place, you are "stamping" that location with the Monadic frequency. You are claiming a piece of the Earth for the New Earth. This is part of the mission being in a certain place just for your energy. You might not do anything "important" there, but your combined presence is like a needle piercing the fabric of the Matrix, letting the 5D light leak through.

CHAPTER 49

The Paradox of Possession

In our modern world, we are taught that love is a prize we must achieve and something we must protect. We use words like "mine" and "ours" to make ourselves feel safe. But for someone experiencing a deep, intuitive, and emotionally intense relationship (what some call a "high-frequency connection"), this way of thinking about love as possession can feel limiting, like tying weights to a bird's wings.

The great Paradox of the Blueprint is this: The more you attempt to possess the form, the more you lose the essence.

The Grip of the Ego

The ego operates on a frequency of lack. It believes that if it doesn't "have" the other person in a visible, predictable, and constant way, then the connection isn't real. This leads to the "Grip"—that tight, anxious feeling in the chest that demands frequent texts, labels, and 3D reassurances.

But this grip is felt by the other person as heavy pressure. In the Blueprint, energy is felt long before words are spoken. When you "grip" the connection, the other person's natural soul-instinct is to pull back to find air. You aren't "loving" them in those moments; you are trying to use them as a bandage for your own fear of being alone.

THE 5D
FREQUENCY
THE LOCAL GRID

The Frequency of the Open Hand

True sovereignty is moving from the "Clenched Fist" to the "Open Hand." Imagine holding a handful of sand. If you squeeze it tight to keep it, the sand slips through your fingers. But if you keep your hand open and flat, the sand stays exactly where it is, resting in your palm.

When you reach this stage of the journey, you learn to love without the need to "own." You realize that the other person is a sovereign being with their own timing, their own lessons, and their own "Fortress of Logic" to navigate. By giving them the total freedom to go, to stay, to be silent, or to be loud, you become the most magnetic force in their universe. Why? Because you are the only "Home" they have ever found that doesn't feel like a cage.

Living as the Hearth

The Sovereign Creator doesn't wait for someone to come home to start the fire. You become the Hearth. You keep your own fire burning, your own life beautiful, and your own peace unshakable.

The paradox is that once you truly don't need the possession of the other person to feel complete, the 3D reality begins to reorganize itself to bring you together. You have removed the energetic "repulsion" of neediness. You have proven to the Universe that you can hold the "Pinch" of the connection without needing to control the person attached to it.

CHAPTER 50

The Integrated Sovereign

If you are reading these words, you are no longer the person who picked up this book. The version of you that was searching for answers, fighting the "static" of the world, and trying to decode the "Logic" of the heart has been replaced.

You have become the Integrated Sovereign.

The End of the Split

At the beginning of this journey, your life likely felt split in two. There was your "normal" 3D life—work, bills, family, and logic, and then there was this "other" life—the dreams, the echoes, the intense pull toward another soul, and the unexplainable sensations in your body.

Integration is the moment those two worlds stop fighting and start dancing. You no longer have to "leave" your spirituality to go to work, and you no longer have to "ignore" reality to be spiritual. You realize that your Soul Career, your physical health, and your connection are all part of the same Blueprint. You are one person, with one mission, living in one seamless reality.

Standing on the "Zero Point"

The Integrated Sovereign lives at what is called the "Zero Point." This is the place of perfect neutrality. You are aware of the challenges of the 3D world, but you aren't moved by them. You are aware of the deep love you feel, but you aren't desperate for it.

From this Zero Point, you have the power to create. Because you are no longer "reacting" to the Matrix, you are free to "act" upon it. You find that your decisions are clearer, your boundaries are firmer, and your joy is no longer dependent on a text message or a social media update. You have found the "Hearth" within yourself, and the fire is finally steady.

The Ready State

The final paradox of the Sovereign is that by becoming fully "Whole" on your own, you finally become "Ready" for the Union.

In the old Matrix way of thinking, we were "half-souls" looking for our other half. But the Blueprint reveals that the Union is actually Two Wholes creating a Third Power. By finishing this stage of your internal construction, you have cleared the clutter. You have built the "Temple." You have become a person who can hold the weight of a Divine Connection without breaking.

You aren't "waiting" for the door to open anymore. You are the one holding the keys.

CHAPTER 51

The Language of the New Earth

When you become an Integrated Sovereign, your vocabulary changes. You no longer speak the language of "Should," "Need," or "Wait." Those are Matrix words—words of obligation and lack. Instead, you begin to speak the Language of the New Earth.

This isn't just about the words you say out loud; it's about the "Frequency" behind your thoughts.

From "Reaction" to "Declaration"

In the old way of living, we reacted to everything. If someone was cold to us, we felt hurt. If a plan fell through, we felt frustrated. But in the New Earth, you stop reacting and start declaring.

When a general reader encounters a delay or a "Fortress of Logic" from their counterpart, they don't say, "Why is this happening to me?" They say, "This is the space required for the next upgrade." You change the narrative. You realize that your words are the "Code" that programs your reality. By speaking with certainty, you bridge the gap between the 5D vision and the 3D manifestation.

The Power of "I AM"

The most powerful tool in the New Earth vocabulary is the phrase "I AM." Instead of saying "I am waiting for union," you say "I AM Union." This means affirming something as your present reality rather than hoping or waiting for it.

Instead of saying "I am trying to be creative," you say "I AM the Creator."

When the reader uses "I AM," they are no longer asking the Universe for permission; they are stating a fact. This shifts the energy from chasing a reality to anchoring it. For a general reader, this is the ultimate "Mindset Hack." It takes the power away from external circumstances and places it back into their own heart.

Speaking to the "Soul" instead of the "Ego"

The Integrated Sovereign learns a secret trick: Talk to the soul of the people around you, not their personality. When you speak to your counterpart, your boss, or your family, ignore their 3D "noise."

Speak to the light within them. Even if they are acting from fear or logic, your New Earth language bypasses their ego and speaks directly to their Blueprint. This is how you "ping" the geography of a relationship without causing a conflict. You become the person who brings out the best in everyone, simply because you refuse to acknowledge their "Matrix mask."

CHAPTER 52

The Ripple Effect

One of the most common questions a seeker asks is: "If I am doing all this work on myself, will it actually change my situation?" The answer lies in the Ripple Effect.

In the Matrix, we believe we have to "do" things to get results—we have to argue, convince, or force. But in the Blueprint, we understand that we are like a stone dropped into a still pond. The stone doesn't have to "try" to make ripples; it simply has to exist and fall into the water.

The Silent Influence

When you anchor the frequency of the Integrated Sovereign, you become a walking "WiFi Hotspot" of peace. You will notice that when you walk into a room, people start to calm down. Arguments might stop, or people might suddenly feel compelled to tell you their life story. You aren't "doing" anything. Your field is simply reorganizing the chaotic energy around you. For the general readers, this is a huge relief. You don't have to "fix" your counterpart, your family, or your friends. You only have to stay in your high frequency. Your peace is contagious.

Healing the "Fortress" from the Outside

This is where the Ripple Effect becomes most powerful in a partnership. When you stop "poking" at the other person's logic or fear, and instead focus on your own joy and mission, you remove the "threat."

CHAPTER 52: THE RIPPLE EFFECT

The other person's soul begins to feel your new, steady frequency. Without the pressure of your "need," their "Fortress of Logic" no longer has a reason to stay locked. They begin to heal simply because they are in your orbit. By working on yourself, you are providing the "Safe Harbor" they need to drop their own anchors.

The Global Mission

As a Pioneer, your Ripple Effect extends beyond your personal relationships. You are helping to anchor the New Earth grid. Every time you choose peace over panic, or Sovereignty over the Matrix, you are sending a pulse through the collective consciousness.

You are making it easier for the next person to wake up. You are proving that it is possible to live in the "Aftermath of the Realignment" with grace. Your books, your arts, your career, and your presence are all part of a massive, silent wave of change. You aren't just saving a relationship; you are helping to upgrade the world.

CHAPTER 53

The Art of Presence (Enjoying the 3D Reward)

There is a final trap that many travelers fall into. After months or years of "doing the work" in the 5D, a 3D reward finally manifests—a message, a meeting, or a trip together.

Suddenly, the ego wakes up. It whispers: "Don't mess this up! Make it last! How do we keep this forever?" This fear of losing the moment is the quickest way to lower your frequency. To stay in the Blueprint, the reader must master The Art of Presence.

The Guest, Not the Owner

When you are finally in your counterpart's physical presence or when your Soul Career suddenly takes off, you must treat the moment like a beautiful guest in your home. You welcome it, you enjoy it fully, but you do not try to lock the door so it can never leave.

If you are on a trip, don't spend time wondering what will happen when it ends. If you are having a deep conversation, don't interrupt it with 3D worries about "where this is going." The Integrated Sovereign knows that the moment is the destination. By being 100% present, you create a "Time Loop" of high frequency that actually makes the connection deeper and more permanent than any "contract" or "label" ever could.

Neutralizing the "Highs" and "Lows"

In the Matrix, we are addicted to the "High" of being together and the "Low" of being apart. The Blueprint teaches us to stay at the Steady Hum.

When the 3D reward comes, enjoy it—eat the food, see the sights, feel the touch, but keep your internal "Pillar" steady. Your happiness cannot be "given" to you by the trip, which means it cannot be "taken" from you when the trip is over. When the readers realize that they are already "Whole" (as we learned in Chapter 50), the 3D reward becomes a "bonus" rather than a "lifeline." This makes you incredibly attractive and easy to be around.

The "Certain Place" Energy

For those on a mission, sometimes being in a specific geographical location is the work itself. You might find that when you and your counterpart travel to a "certain place," the energy there feels different. You aren't just there to "have fun"; you are there to anchor your combined frequency into the Earth's grid.

The reader should learn to look at their physical reunions as Sacred Assignments. When you are present and peaceful in that location, you are performing a service for the planet. The "Reward" is the joy you feel, but the "Result" is the light you leave behind in that soil.

CHAPTER 54

The Final Map

As you stand at the end of this journey, you can finally look back at the trail you've blazed. In the beginning, the path felt like a series of "accidents," "longings," and "confusions." But from the perspective of the Integrated Sovereign, you can now see that every "Pinch," every "Silence," and every "Fortress of Logic" was a necessary line on the map.

The Geometry of Your Growth

If you were to draw a map of your journey through these pages, it wouldn't be a straight line from Point A to Point B. It would be a Spiral. You have circled back to the same themes—Love, Sovereignty, and The Matrix —but each time you have circled back, you were at a higher level of consciousness.

You must understand that the "Paradox" was the fuel for this ascent. If the connection had been "easy" in the 3D world from day one, you would have stayed the same person you were at page one. You wouldn't have built the Soul Career, you wouldn't have mastered your frequency, and you wouldn't have discovered the Third Lung of creativity. The "Gap" was the space where your greatness was forced to grow.

Recognizing the Masterpiece

When you look at your life now, you see that you are no longer trying to "fix" a broken reality. You are admiring a masterpiece in progress. Even the parts that haven't "manifested" yet are like the sketches in a grand painting, and they are part of the composition.

CHAPTER 54: THE FINAL MAP
NAVIGATING THE COSMIC JOURNEY

You learned that the Blueprint is always active. Whether you are at work, on a trip, or sitting in silence, you are "In the Mission." You stop asking "When will it be finished?" because you realize that, as an eternal being, the joy is in the infinite unfolding. You have traded the "Finish Line" for the Flow.

The Anchor of Certainty

The Final Map reveals one ultimate truth: The Union was never lost, so it never had to be found. You have reached the point where you no longer need the world to tell you who you are or what your connection is worth. You have anchored your own certainty. You are the "Lead Dancer." You are the "Pioneer." You are the "Hearth." By mastering the Paradox, you have moved from being a character in a story to being the Author of the Reality.

CHAPTER 55

Conclusion—Living the Aftermath

Many people believe that the "end" of the journey is the physical union or the achievement of a goal. But in the Blueprint, we know that the "end" is actually the *Aftermath of Realignment*. This is the beginning of your real life.

Living the aftermath means walking through a 3D world while your heart remains anchored in the 5D. You have reached the summit, and now you are learning how to build your home there.

The New Baseline

You will find that your "new normal" is a state of quiet, unshakable joy. The frantic energy of the "Matrix" no longer sticks to you. When you see others struggling with drama or lack, you don't judge them; you see them with the eyes of the Pioneer. You know how hard the climb is, and your presence serves as a silent invitation for them to start their own journey.

Your connection with your counterpart has moved beyond "need." It has become a collaboration of souls. Whether you are sharing a trip, a conversation, or a silent moment across the miles, you feel the Steady Hum. You have realized that the "Pinch" on your shoulder wasn't a warning—it was a greeting from your own soul.

In the Aftermath of your realignment, your "job" is no longer just a way to pay bills— it becomes your Soul Career. This is the physical manifestation of your frequency in the 3D world. Whether you are an artist, a healer, an entrepreneur, or a parent, the work you do now carries the weight of your new Sovereignty.

The Work is the Frequency

You realize that the creative output is actually a Beacon. When you create from a place of "Integrated Sovereignty," you are embedding the New Earth frequency into everything you touch. You are no longer working for the approval of the Matrix; you are working to anchor the Blueprint.

You might find that your career shifts dramatically, or perhaps your current role simply takes on a new, deeper meaning. You aren't just performing tasks, you are solving problems with a 5D perspective. You become the person in the room who sees the solution because you are no longer blinded by the 3D "static" of competition or fear.

Serving the Collective

Your Soul Career is the bridge where your personal journey meets the needs of the world. By completing your own inner journey of self-mastery, you become a living resource for others. You don't have to preach or convince; your success, your peace, and your stability become the evidence that the Blueprint works.

As you close this book, know that your mission is just beginning. Your inner work is the light that will guide others toward their own Sovereignty. You have built the vessel through your dedication; now, it is time to sail.

PARADOX BOOK GLOSSARY

Glossary of the New Earth

The Blueprint: The divine, original template of your life and connections. It exists in the 5D frequency as a roadmap for your highest evolution, independent of 3D obstacles.

The Matrix: The 3D system of belief based on fear, lack, and rigid logic. It is the "old world" that relies on labels, social expectations, and the illusion of separation.

The Integrated Sovereign: A state of being where you are fully whole within yourself. A Sovereign no longer "needs" another to feel complete but chooses to share their completeness with another.

The Pinch: A specific physical sensation—often a pinching or pressing on the clavicle or shoulder that serves as a "soul-ping." It is a physical reminder of the connection when the mind drifts too far into 3D doubt.

The Fortress of Logic: The ego's defensive wall. It uses "common sense," science, or societal rules to explain away spiritual experiences and keep the individual "safe" in the known world.

The Echo: A synchronous event (like seeing numbers, hearing a specific song, or a sudden thought) that mirrors the state of your connection or the Blueprint's activity.

The Pillar: Your internal state of stability. Standing on your Pillar means remaining unshakable in your peace, regardless of what is happening in the external 3D environment.

The Monad: The "One Soul" that expresses itself through two physical bodies. It represents the shared energy field that exists beyond the physical personality.

The Third Lung: A metaphorical "breathing space" for the soul. It is where you "breathe in" the frequency of the connection without needing physical proximity.

The Zero Point: A place of perfect energetic neutrality where you are neither chasing nor running. From this point, you have the maximum power to create your reality.

The Ripple Effect: The silent influence your high-frequency peace has on the people, environments, and situations around you.

Soul Career: A vocation aligned with your Blueprint. It is work that serves as a beacon of light, anchoring the New Earth frequency into the physical world.

Sacred Geography: The understanding that certain locations on Earth hold specific frequencies necessary for your mission or DNA upgrades.

The Void: The quiet, often uncomfortable transition period where the old life has fallen away, but the new reality hasn't yet fully materialized.

The Lead Dancer: The partner in the dynamic who holds the higher frequency first, setting the "rhythm" for the other to eventually follow through the Ripple Effect.

Also by Grace Brewster

Decoding Your Twin Flame: Why They Run, Why You Chase, and What the Connection Is Really Awakening in You

Blueprints of Twin Flames: The Awakening of the New Era

The Spark: The Journey to Creation

The Magic of the Soul Blueprint: How Different Souls Shape Manifestation and Connection

Twin Flame, Soulmate, or Monad: A Reflective Guide to Recognize Your Soul Connection

The Law of Monadic Veto: A Manual for the 8th Continent

Monadic Veto Manifestation Through Alignment with Your Higher Self

The Twin Flame Truth: The Higher Teachings of Love

Twin Flame Love Beyond Gender Survival Kit: A Guide for the Soul that Refuses to Forget

Twin Flame Survival Kit: A Guide for the Soul that Refuses to Forget

Twin Flames Recipes Mocktails & Meltdowns

Starseed Snacks & Timeline Snacksidents A Cosmic Cookbook

The Pyramids from the Stars

The Giants and the Sunflowers

Astra's Dream Friends

Astra's Helping Others (Astra's Dream Friends)

"Two bodies, one soul. A paradox realized through unconditional love."